THE
COMMON
TABLE

ALSO BY THE AUTHOR
Small Decencies

THE COMMON TABLE

*Reflections and
Meditations
on Community
and Spirituality
in the
Workplace*

JOHN COWAN

HarperBusiness
A Division of HarperCollins*Publishers*

HarperCollins books may be purchased for educational, business, or sales promotional use. For information please write: Special Markets Department, HarperCollins Publishers, Inc., 10 East 53rd Street, New York, NY 10022.

FIRST EDITION

Designed by C. Linda Dingler

Library of Congress Cataloging-in-Publication Data

Cowan, John, 1935–
      The common table : reflections and meditations on community and spirituality in the workplace / John Cowan. — 1st ed.
          p.   cm.
      ISBN 0-88730-649-7
      1. Business ethics. 2. Management—Moral and ethical aspects. 3. Spiritual life. I. Title.
      HF5387.C678   1993
      174'.4—dc20   92-56235

93 94 95 96 97 ❖/HC 10 9 8 7 6 5 4 3 2 1

CONTENTS

INTRODUCTION

———— ✕ ————

IN MY LAST BOOK, SMALL DECENCIES, I WROTE ABOUT THE
feeling of leaving home for my first day of school as a little kid and never coming back. The system grabbed me,
as it has grabbed many others, pounded me with negative
feedback, and tried to get me to be somebody I was not.
The first thing I learned at school was that I was to no
longer be left-handed because school desks were built for
right-handed people. The essay was entitled "For the
Children." I was sad for all children, that this kind of reg-
imentation had to happen to them. That they could not
live a life filled with the praise they deserve, for we all are
marvelous creatures.

Since that book was published, I have had the chance
to come home, at least partially. My life has been filled
with praise. People from around the country have
thanked me for the book and for being myself. This has
been very nice, and I am thankful for it.

I hope that you can have this experience in your own
way. I hope people crowd around you and tell you you are
the most efficient clerical in the company, the wisest
executive, the strongest laborer, the most sympathetic
ear, the best dresser, the quickest programmer, the kindest
father, or the most thoughtful lover, that you have the
most skilled wrench, the cutest round belly, the hand-
somest beard, or that you shine at whatever it is that is
your talent.

If you have not read *Small Decencies*, I suggest that you
read it before reading this book. It was written more from

my feminine side, the more agreeable side of my personality. *The Common Table* comes more from the masculine side and is a little tougher and more forceful. The difference is subtle, but I noticed that in the first book I write quite a bit about my mother, and in this one I write much more about my father. Last time I talked more about business and the heart and this time I talk a little more about where I think we businesspeople should be going.

I would like to write a third book in this series, and it may come, but I cannot guarantee it. Most writers who embark on this kind of endeavor seem to go downhill gradually at the same time as they provoke more critical interest. I have been praised in the *Highland Villager*, and I don't intend to end by being panned in *The New York Times*.

On the other hand, I have had a recent dream in which I was playing the trumpet, something I cannot do in real life, and playing it rather well, except that I was using only two of the keys, both brass-tipped. There was a silver-tipped key that I was not using, and in the back of my mind while dreaming was the thought that I could learn to play the bugle and that that would be an even better idea than playing the trumpet. So maybe someday I will find a way to press the silver key, or I may gather my courage and play the bugle, and there will be a third book—although the bugle is a difficult instrument for a man who keeps his real intentions secret and is accustomed to sneaking up on all destinations from the side. We must just wait and see.

I thank Jean Freeman, Jerri Fosdick, John Johnson, Jay Hanson, and Dick Leider for giving support, against all reason, to a very strange man; Dick Byrd for providing the tension that moved me away from one comfortable pole and left me hanging, kicking, and screaming quite creatively, out in the abyss somewhere; Sandra Merwin for telling me what my dreams might mean; Margaret Wimberger for copyediting this with one hand while tending to a newborn baby with the other; Virginia Smith for pouncing upon my manuscript and advocating it within HarperCollins; Jonathon Lazear for becoming my agent and contacting a business editor with a most unlikely proposal; Edith, my wife, who is the best companion this man can have for any journey, particularly the journey of life; and my sons for providing both stories and meaning.

It is a nice day, isn't it? I cannot prevent myself from having the feelings I used to have in the early sixties: that I am living in a time of sea change and am part of some movement much bigger than myself. Riding into battle, some Indian warriors used to say to one another, "It is a good day to die." I amend that to say, "It is a good day to live."

JOHN COWAN

on a snowy day in
St. Paul, Minnesota, 1993

THE
COMMON
TABLE

GOOD LINES

I USUALLY WAIT A WHILE BEFORE I PASS THIS ON TO NEO-phyte sailors. I think it shocks them when we leave the harbor and I give them the tiller, never to take it back unless they decide they don't like piloting the boat. I give them a while to get used to what the wind does, how the boat behaves, and what they must do before I say: "If we get hit by a gust, the boat will tip way over on its side. You'll be tempted to turn into the wind to straighten it out. Don't! Hold the rudder steady. Keep pressure on. The boat has good lines. She was designed to turn herself up into the wind in heavy gusts. She will not tip all the way over."

The advice does little good. The first blast hits and the women squeak and the men get a paralyzed what-am-I-doing-wrong expression on their faces. I reach back and usually just touch the tiller with a finger or two, enough to let them know that I know what's happening and there is no cause for panic. They hold firm, and the *Laughing Buddha* leans to her side, comes up throwing water from her rail, and then, with the rudder pressure steady, turns herself back down, snorting defiance at a wind that thought it could scare off a rock-solid boat like her.

I have great faith in human beings. Some people have faith in humans because they believe in God; I believe in God because I have watched human beings and have developed a faith in them. I don't understand people who believe in God and don't believe in people. That is not to say that everybody does the right thing always. It is in the long haul and in the larger order that I believe in people.

Carl Rogers, during the fifties, created a type of counseling dedicated to complete noninterference with the client. The counselor was to simply reflect back whatever the client said, complete with emotional content, in a tone of voice that conveyed acceptance of the client and faith that the client had the capacity to change. I'm not in that field anymore, but it seems those who are don't do it Carl's way these days. I think I later heard that even Carl modified his approach. But in my experience as a counselor, it worked. People improved, grew, recreated their lives right from inside themselves. Maybe they've come up with something that works better, but the success of this approach seemed to me to indicate that people will struggle toward the good, and they will get there if they are given time and love.

My present profession is organization development. Like a doctor, I am usually not called until things are bad. I have been invited into some extremely painful, even crazy, situations. My first step is to interview everyone concerned, and write up what I hear. My second step is to gather everyone together, have them read my notes, and then have them as a group tell me sentence by sentence where I have recorded the situation accurately, where I am mistaken, and if I am mistaken, what the truth of the matter is. When they have agreed to the situation, I then ask them to fix it. And usually they do. The worse the situation, the better they fix it.

It is harder for me to be confident about nations and the world as a whole working out their problems. But it seems to me that I have seen the same pattern in history as I have seen in groups and individuals and good boats. Hitler came, but he has been defeated. Jesus was crucified, but his ways have conquered. Polio was a scourge, but we are on top of it. I live better than my father could have. And I think we will keep creating a better and better world. Sometimes we will fall back, and sometimes we will err. But on the whole, we will progress.

So I sit somewhat comfortably this year, knowing that poverty in our country has grown, not decreased, over the last years, and that our cities are close to explosion. I know that our businesses are still sexist, racist, oriented toward power over the many by the few, contributing to an ongoing unfair distribution of the wealth both in our work force and throughout the world. Yet I am comfortable because I am certain that we will do something about all of this. Maybe not tomorrow, but we will do it. Indeed, I plan to remain devoted to the cause, as are many, many others.

I bought a new rudder. I was standing by the pull-out ramp attaching it when one of my A-Dock neighbors came by. He had been sailing and told me that it was a strange day out there. He had been knocked down twice in succession, once from either side. The wind is not supposed to be like that. I was sympathetic, but not attentive. I was focused on wrenches and nuts and bolts, the kind of task I am not very good at.

With the rudder attached, I took the *Laughing Buddha* for a test run. The wind was mild, but fitful and erratic. It kept shifting on me as I raised the sails. But then it steadied, and I enjoyed the feel of the new rudder. The boat was faster. Nick down at Seaward had redesigned the rudder, and I could feel it hold the boat on a straighter course. I saw the gust coming and thought little of it except that now I would get to feel how the rudder would respond to a little wind. Instead of watching the gust, I looked back at the tiller to be sure that I kept it steady and that the boat's response would be a function of the new rudder, not of my ability to adjust. The boat began to tip, and I looked backward. And then it continued to tip and I looked forward to see the bellying genoa about to touch the waves. As I grabbed a stanchion to keep from falling off, my feet scrabbling for purchase against the cockpit side, water began to pour into the boat. Never have I taken water into the cockpit of a keel boat, and never have I been hit with that much wind with all my sails up.

I was tempted to release the tiller, push it away, and turn the boat into the wind, but I gave myself the novice's speech. "Hold her steady. She is a good boat with great lines. She will come up."

She did.

So will we.

THE COMMON TABLE

THIS YEAR WE WILL BE GOING BACK TO CAMP, THE CASS Lake Episcopal Camp, "up on the res'," as the Indians say. I remember the first time I took my family up there, dread gaining on dread as I drove the last few miles. "What am I in for?" I thought, "Religion dripping from the trees? Prayer services morning, noon, and night? Sanctimonious saps uttering pious platitudes?"

It wasn't like that. There were some prayers, but not too many. There was some religious discussion, but not too much. There were a couple of pious souls, but not too sappy. And there was that which brought me back year after year—the common table.

The mess hall is a rudimentary building: one level, with a concrete floor, windows opening from the bottom and hinged at the top, and the framework showing from the inside. About a quarter of the space is walled off for a kitchen, and fourteen tables and twenty-eight backless benches are lined across the room in double rows with a center aisle. There is a stone fireplace opposite the kitchen.

That first evening, after my little Datsun was unloaded of kids and gear, my family and I cautiously entered, sizing up the situation, meeting the cautious stares of other new families, beginning the sniffing-and-feeling-out procedure. As a family we timidly made our way through the line, carefully sought a table for ourselves, and ringed a corner to exclude whoever else might intrude on the safety of our circle. Thawing out began with meeting the

next family down the table, continued over the crazy
songs and introductions, and flourished over the camp-
fire.

At breakfast the next day, I lost my six-year-old son to
the counselors' table. At lunch I lost my four-year-old to
the table of the four-year-old girl in the next cabin, and
at supper I lost my wife to the women's Bemidji woolen-
mills shopping-tour planning group. By the next day I
considered it a great coincidence if I ate with any of my
own family. It was a delight to discuss philosophy with
the Carleton College professor, painting with the hippie
couple from the inner city, or finance with the broker, or
to feed someone else's baby because it was parked in a
high chair three feet from my elbow. By the middle of the
week a stranger could not have told from the mess hall
seating who belonged to whom. We had learned to eat at
the common table.

We had driven in at different hours during the Sunday
arrival period. After unloading, everyone had parked
their cars nose into the bushes in the parking area a little
distance from the camp proper. The cars would seldom be
used during the week. For amusement one day, I tried to
guess which car belonged to whom. Whose was the new
BMW? The ancient Chevy? Who owned the battered
pickup truck? The slick Suburban? I am happy to report
that at the end of the week, as people reloaded their cars,
I discovered that I had not guessed right once. Nothing
had happened all week to let me know who was rich or
who was poor.

When our stay at the camp ended, it was a shock to
return to the real world of work, although I adapted
quickly for the sake of survival. The BMWs rolled into
the executive garage. The Datsuns and Chevys circled
the outside of the office building, the battered pickups
pulled up to the factory. The factory people did not dare
come over to the office cafeteria, although it was close

and far superior to theirs. Executives ate in the executive dining room, where other professionals below a certain grade were not allowed. Nobody would have the slightest difficulty knowing who belonged where. We all dressed for our own station in life. Salary ranges could be accurately discerned from the cut of the cloth and from the bolt from which the cloth had been cut.

Some people did try to break the norm. Even the chairman of the board tried. When management told Bill that it was going to build an executive dining room, he refused to authorize it, saying he didn't know why other executives couldn't eat with the ordinary folk. He himself brought a brown bag from home instead of breaking for lunch.

Even the chairman of the board's will and intention can be subverted. Management came back to him with the request for a "guest dining room," which he approved. Then, since we seldom had guests, the room filled with executives. Then, since he was no longer paying attention, the sign on the door was changed to "Executive Dining Room" to make it clear that peons were not welcome.

The executive dining room was as stiff as I imagine the Queen of England's formal dining table to be. I have known people to refuse to enter it because they were wearing the wrong suit. People reported to me that they were uncomfortable being observed by other executives lest they do something clumsy or inappropriate. Certainly, the conversation at every table I ever sat at in there began with a review of who was sitting with whom and what the significance of that might be.

Since a corporation is not a church camp but a pragmatic place, existing for the sake of the bottom line, I could accept it as a fair argument that these dining customs were justifiable because they increased effectiveness. But in actuality, I never noticed that to be the case. We did not work well together. We did not actively care for one another's well-being. The professionals on my level gave grudging obedience to the occupants of the executive dining room, denigrating their wisdom behind their backs. They in turn were much more entranced with exercising their own power than with seeking the results of our skills or knowledge. There was ample evidence that executives were willing in their decision making to protect their own good and let one another quietly drown.

There is at least one scholar of the Christian scriptures who says that the reason Jesus of Nazareth angered the authorities enough to be crucified was that he ate at a common table. That was the sin for which he had to be punished, the cause of the accusations that he fomented trouble. He acted as if the rich were on the same level as the poor, the good wife on the same level as the prostitute, the landowner and the heretic equally welcome to use similar utensils.

As the legend goes, the Chinese philosopher Lao-tzu, leaving the city in disgust, was stopped by the gatekeeper and asked to leave his wisdom in writing so that the city would at least know what he was disgusted at. He wrote the *Tao Te Ching*, a poem to leaders insisting that they make themselves lower than their followers.

The original Buddha found himself the bearer of the Buddha nature only after he set aside the trappings of the prince.

So twenty centuries and more after these world religion founders ran this idea up the flagpole, it still is not selling too well. Maybe it's a bad idea. Maybe we just can't function that way. Maybe the change of heart is too much to ask. Maybe the powerful have to have a special club to retire to or society will fall apart absent the deals that are cooked up there. All this is possible. But I ask myself, Why do I return to my immaculate work scene feeling distinctly uncomfortable? And why, when I am looking for a vacation, do I aim for Bemidji, for Cass Lake, for the noisy ruckus of carrying a tray of macaroni and cheese to the melting pot of the common table?

Could it be that that is precisely where human beings belong?

THE LOSING TEAM

THE HIGHLAND-CENTRAL HOCKEY TEAM LOST TO COMO High School, and I cannot tell you how bad that made me feel. I came to the game hoping for much better. For the last three years we have had a good chance against Como, winning about half the time. What I had forgotten is that three years ago Como fielded mostly freshmen, and then mostly sophomores, and then (and they won both times), mostly juniors, and finally now twelve seniors, pretty good ones at that.

We are not a very good team, and we will lose more conference games than we will win, but it is Humboldt and Como that we will beat if we beat anyone. Our first conference game was against Humboldt, and we cleaned their clocks. This was only our second conference game, and Como humiliated us. From here we face the better teams. We are downward bound. For three years I have watched my son Ben fight the valiant fight in a losing cause. This year I had hoped for at least a little better, but I guess it is simply not in the cards. I would like him to experience a winning high school season, but I am afraid it is not going to happen. I guess he will survive this. He was much more cheerful about the defeat than I was. God knows, playing on a losing team is a part of life.

My last losing team was an operation called Business Advisors, set up by Control Data with a mission to sell our extensive internal corporate staff talent to other companies. Our executives' minds were clouded by the desperate need to reduce overhead without firing 150 talented members of corporate staff. My bosses made a mistake, but their intentions were honorable. Their mistake gave me the chance to learn some lessons about being on a losing team, lessons I noticed Ben putting into practice last night.

Keep playing the game. There is a temptation to quit. This is not a good idea. Against Como, Ben banged into more people, stole more pucks, made more brilliant passes than he did against Humboldt. Anything less and the team is truly humiliated, injury becomes more likely, and after the game, sleep comes more slowly.

Don't try to do what you can't. Against Humboldt Ben was an extremely aggressive defenseman. I suggested to him that normally people playing his position follow their front line down the ice, rather than lead it. Against Como, when playing defense, he played defense. In a losing business the temptation is to play all the roles, from manager to secretary. First of all, it can't be done. Second, if you try it, everybody else quits working. Third, if you are doing their jobs, is anyone doing yours?

Redefine winning. Como caught me by surprise. Next time I will feel better, because next time "winning" will be defined as losing 5–2 instead of 8–1. In a losing situation, thinking that you are about to pull off an extraordinary victory leads to disastrous activities. You forget, as three of our defensemen kept forgetting in the heat of attacking, that Como had several players who could outskate them. Or as Business Advisors forgot, in the heat of packaging our brilliant corporate staff work, that our customers had their own corporate staffs who thought that they were brilliant also and therefore were somewhat resistant to buying from us.

Use your resources judiciously. For decades the winning Control Data threw money at problems. You can't do that when you are losing. Ben is a highly skilled hockey player. (Others say that too.) His coach used him at defense, center, and wing. I recommend that when clearly losing he use Ben at defense only. It is an effective form of damage control. Don't put your best resources into attack when attack is futile.

Enjoy every minute of it. Hey, beating Humboldt was easy. Stemming the blood when playing Como is challenging. Although doing good is always difficult, anybody can *look* good managing the upswing. It takes talent to operate when the shit is hitting the fan. You said you liked challenge. Here it is.

Prepare for your next move. Eventually a losing business will be disbanded. (For Ben's sake, I wish that were true of a losing hockey team.) Prepare for a safe transition. At Business Advisors I started a newsletter more than seven years ago to assure the business community we were available. I also wanted it to know I was around for the day that Business Advisors failed. That is why the newsletter was called *A Jotting from John* and not some more corporate-sounding name.

It is more fun playing on a winning team. But if you are willing to work a little harder, being on a losing team can have its own rewards. If you play the game hard enough, you may even win!

CLIFF'S EDGE

———— ✕ ————

IT IS A FUNNY WORLD WE WHITE-COLLAR TYPES LIVE IN.

On the Wisconsin side of Lake Pepin, just south of Maidenrock (population 103), county road AA leaves the lake and winds up into the hills. Suddenly it breaks from the trees, and if you are driving up there, you find yourself on huge flat farmland. The feeling is spacious. Miles of rolling freedom unfold before you. Farther to the east, silo towers lift above the tree line. To the west, if you cut back toward the lake, the land remains flat, until the final moment when you pull your car to a stop on the edge of a sheer cliff.

I am not good at judging these things, but I think it's about a three-hundred-foot drop. At one moment I and my four-wheel-drive could turn in any direction with complete safety, and the next, I am stepping out of my truck with eerie feelings of acrophobia: one misstep and I'm in freefall, soon to be dead.

A young priest friend of mine took over temporary responsibility for the most affluent Episcopal church in the state of Minnesota. He was puzzled by church meetings. On the surface all was well: a perfectly fine group of well-to-do people doing their best to do what was best. But he had the feeling something was going on that he couldn't understand. Unable to bear the ambiguity any longer, he asked an older priest who had been associated with the parish for several years what it was that he was sensing but could not name.

The older priest said, "Try the word *fear*."

That was it! Everything made sense if he took as his basic assumption that most of these folks were scared out of their wits. Sure, they were well-to-do. They were presidents of this and vice presidents of that, leading politicians, income-producing brokers, insurance agents, restaurateurs. They owned expensive cars, homes with pools, club memberships, condominiums in Aspen, and homes in Florida, and they were all scared silly because they lived on the edge of the cliff. One mistake, one change in management, one recessionary cycle, and the paycheck that supported all that wealth could slip away, sending them tumbling down a financial cliff and causing them to lose the accoutrements of their life-style and along with that their right to belong to their community of friends. Frayed collars and secondhand dresses weren't appreciated at this church.

It's a funny world we white-collar professionals live in—ostensibly on the fat flatland but really on the edge of the precipice.

My friend found a way to live in this church. When he wanted rest, he sought refuge not at the quarter-million-dollar home but at the two-bedroom rambler. When he wanted judicious opinion, he sought it not from pinstripe suits but from the people with run-down heels. He found some people in the parish who were living below their means, under their station, nursing a rainy-day fund and unafraid of being shoved off the precipice. They had pitched their tent a mile back from the edge.

That is not a bad idea.

A LITTLE YOGA IS A
GOOD THING

I HAVE JUST STARTED YOGA. I AM AT MY TENTH LESSON AND am enjoying it very much. The tenth lesson has been a critical time for me ever since I arrived at my tenth flying lesson and realized that the instructor was overdue to let me fly the plane alone and might be feeling that he should have me do so despite the fact that I was unlikely to land it successfully. I was quite good at taking off, but since landing does seem to me an integral part of the process, I simply did not come back for lesson eleven.

I am coming back for lesson eleven in yoga. Not that I am a spectacular practitioner or even student. I am probably thirty years older than the average student and ten years older than anyone in the class. The years make for less flexibility and therefore less accuracy in imitating the posture of my instructor, Faye, even though she does us all the favor of seldom going to the extremes in bending, of which she is supremely capable. But this is not a contest, and my purpose is to enhance self-awareness and increase flexibility, both of which I am achieving, despite the fact that others have displayed more flexibility in the beginning of the course than I will display at the end.

The other day Faye started talking about the position of the head, and though it sounded like nonsense I listened closely because during our first lesson she had spoken about the position of the pelvis and that too sounded like nonsense, but after I had practiced standing correctly for a week, I understood what she was talking about and felt some clear physical relief. She told us that the position of the head was critical to the body's well-being and demonstrated by holding her own head just wrong and adjusting it until it was just right. No one in the class could see the difference. The only change I could see was that when she held her head correctly, she smiled. A little smile. An enormously pleased, even self-satisfied little smile. I did not comment on this because I was already thought of as class clown, a reputation I quickly collect in any gathering of people who do not know me, don't know that I am very thoughtful, and therefore assume that I am very humorous.

Faye gave up on explaining further. My experience in the class had been that if I just tried to do what she says, often I found out what she means. I tried adjusting my head during the intermission of a dance concert I was attending. First I held it a little bit back from its normal position, which obviously was not right, and then I tried it slightly forward. Something popped in my neck. I could feel muscles (I think they were muscles) loosening around my scalp. My back inadvertently straightened. "Why are you smiling?" my wife asked. "Didn't know I was," I responded, too embarrassed to explain the little game I was playing and too satisfied with its effects to risk losing the moment as I explained it.

Frequently I am called in to organizations to fix the employees. I have been doing this for some time, and I can usually put my finger on the problem pretty quickly, but since there is no better way to speed the process than doing what I am asked to do, that is what I do. First, I interview the employees. Then I go to management and tell them that I have identified the problem that has eluded them for years; I have in my possession the key to their success. With one small adjustment their whole organization will pop into line, functioning with much greater health, and readily open to a few other remedies that will make it a model corporation. Without that adjustment all other prescriptions are useless.

They like this idea. They are not quite sure if they should believe me, but they are very ready to hear me. "The one small adjustment to be made," I say, "is an adjustment in the way you manage people. We need to adjust your head."

They don't like that.

I do say it much more politely than I have said it here. I sneak up on it. But I say it clearly enough so they hear it, and they don't like it. They would prefer a program that costs ten times as much, as long as it leaves their heads alone.

Not all heads need the same adjustment. Some need to seek employee opinion. Some need to be clear on what they are trying to do. Some need to leave employees more to their own devices. Some need to get their spoon in the stew and do some stirring. Some need to find some compassion in their cold hearts, and some need to find some rational resolve in their fuzzy thinking. But all need to do something they do not naturally do well, and that, almost to the last person, they hate to do.

And yet, who does not need to make adjustments? My yoga instructor listens to her instructors and reports immense gains from her experiences with them.

In business as in yoga, if the head is lined up correctly, the vertebrae will find their proper order. Do you send a corporate trainer to five thousand employees to emphasize the need for quality, or change your own thinking to put quality first, even ahead of revenue? Post your EEO strategies on the wall, or hire a black lesbian CFO who never saw a number she didn't understand? Organize quality circles, or ask everyone around you for their opinions, showing signs in your decision making that you've heard them? In each case the second option is significantly more cost-effective and easier to accomplish, if only the head is willing to adjust the head. Which turns out to be not exactly easy, or more would do it.

You may not be a head. You may be a toe. This I understand quite well. In twenty years of being a church-man and eleven years of being a corporate employee, I was a toe. We toes often feel helpless, unable to improve the organization, condemned to simply complain about it. "After all, I am not the leader."

Some years ago, I used to run for my health. I did it religiously but badly. I was as strong as a horse, but according to one observer, I ran "funny." My weight dropped lower than it should have been. When I first began, I had trouble with my right knee, and then the trouble left the knee and moved to the calf, then to the ankle, and then back to the knee and so on.

My wife offered to pull my toes, a strange, primordial custom probably preserved by her family since the Stone Age, in which the toes are pulled, one at a time, until they click. Her family finds satisfaction in this ritual. In my family, we kept our hands off one another; all body parts were private parts. Now, as I lay on the davenport twisted in pain, I allowed my wife to pull my right little toe, not because I thought it would help but because she would find it satisfying. The toe clicked. My right ankle, calf, and knee loosened into complete relaxation. The pain was gone.

The next day I ran and suffered a little. As I stepped gingerly out of the shower, I reached down and tugged on my little toe. It worked again. And again. And again.

Not all toes need the same adjustment. Some need to stop annoying everyone around them with their constant complaining about things that are just part of work life. Some need to get more aggressive about what they want, because if they were to get it, they and their work would be better for it. Some need to increase their competence with training or coaching. Some need to think bigger, to discover that they could do more than they are doing and enjoy themselves more at the same time. Some need to do less worrying about their careers and more worrying about the task at hand.

I do think adjusting the head will cause the most effect on a corporation, but if you are not a head, adjust what you are. Even if you are only a toe. You may be amazed at how far the ripple effect spreads.

LESSONS FROM THE OLD MAN

BACK AROUND 1980 A COLLEAGUE AND I WENT TO A CON-
ference about men put on by a men's group at a local community college. The corporation paid for us to attend, and
the campus seemed a much nicer place to be on a spring
day than the second floor of our corporate tower. A fair
percentage of the attendees were gay, and I found it helpful to hear how the world looked from their place. Several
attendees were women, so I had the chance to once again
hear how women thought I should be doing the job of
being a man—not an uninteresting view.

On the second afternoon we were invited to attend a
play. It was quite allegorical and poetic, and to the surprise of nearly everyone except myself, I liked it. In it a
man was struggling to tell his son what a man should be,
and a good part of his difficulty was that his own father
had never told him. After the play we were allowed to discuss it with the actors and the author, a privilege of which
I was pleased to take advantage. I enjoyed the discussion.
In the middle of it I commented that I found it sad that
this father had failed to perform so simple a task as telling
his son what a man is. The playwright said that *all* fathers
fail to tell their sons what it means to be a man.

I took a deep breath, intending to argue with her that
many fathers, including my own, did an excellent job of
this. But then I glanced around and saw almost every
head nodding support for her statement, and realized that
once I stepped off this plank, I would have to tell them
what my father had taught me. Remembering the tone of

the conference, I knew that they would not like his lessons one whit and would think me a fool for following them.

My father was no saint. I did not idolize him. So I have not accepted everything he taught me, but certain values have stood the test of time, and I now hold them with determination.

Your family comes first. Men provide for their families. If the wife works, as my mother often did and my wife does, that is well and good. But as a man you are the final rock on which the family's security rests. All worries are ultimately yours. If you have to spend your life at a job you do not like and are not good at so that your children can go to college as you could not because your father died, you will do it, because at the end you will be able to say that you have accomplished the one thing on which a man is judged. You have provided for your family. If your children or your wife are in trouble at any time or in any place, you will set aside whatever you are doing and come to their aid. That is what you are for. You are for them.

Lest you think that this is advice that only men who choose to be fathers of families can follow, I will add that the most convincing example of this ideal followed to its hilt that I have ever seen was in a newspaper portrayal of one gay man taking care of his AIDS-stricken lover and companion. Although his family did not consist of a wife and 2.3 blond-haired kids, when I read that article and looked at the pictures, I said to myself, "That's *it!* Precisely what the old man said we men are built to do."

Men are "for" something. After your family there must be some larger whole, or purpose, for which you live. My father was for the union. He lived it, breathed it, slept it. When the company promoted him from a mechanic to a lobbyist, which made him no longer eligible to be a union man, he began the process of dying. He was no longer living for anything, so why bother living?

In our age many struggle for eternity through youth-preserving exercise, through the healthful diet, through medical miracles. I prefer to seek my eternity by being for something bigger than myself. Therein lies my devotion to my religion, my profession, my family, and my country. They will live when I have died. That's what my father taught me.

You will act and speak the truth. My father did not know much about Gandhi, and what he did know he probably didn't like. Not for him, skinny men wearing weird clothes. Yet he understood Gandhi more than many who claim to follow his principles. Gandhi decided early in life that he himself would be an experiment in truth. He would act and speak the truth and then see what happened. What some have thought of as his clever sociopolitical ruses were not ruses at all. He went to the sea to make salt because, despite the import-encouraging British law against doing so, he knew that everyone in India had a right to make salt. That and a few other acts of truth got him half a lifetime in prison and toppled a huge chunk of the British empire.

When I am told that to get a message across I must be other than myself, play the game the way it is supposed to be played, I remember Gandhi, half-naked among executive suits, saying: "Be your message." And I think of my father, who did not say his message, but was it. As union president he once conceded to the company by withdrawing a two-cent wage increase for his own shop so that everyone in the union would receive half a cent more. For the next month at work, no one would speak to him. If he showed up on a coffee break, they went back to work. If he sat at their table for lunch, they went to another table. He endured much pain but had no regrets. A man speaks and acts the truth.

Be a loyal friend to anyone who will have you. Probably because he was raised in a small town in northern

Minnesota, Charlie said hello to everyone he met and assumed that everyone had a good heart and would like him in return. He drove drunks to Willmar to dry out. He led the cops into his good friend's apartment because he was the only person who could pull the protective dog off his friend's dead body. He pushed snowstuck cars. He returned to Northhome to visit his father's ancient friends.

A man needs friends. A man needs to be a friend. People call me out of the blue to seek help finding jobs. I am not much good at it, but I try, for what else can I do? I am Charlie Cowan's son.

If someone insists on attacking you, fight him. Teach the world that you are a nice guy because you choose to be, not because you are too cowardly to be anything else. A man is not a person to be trifled with. If your enemy floors you, gnaw on his ankle until he gives up. If you floor your enemy, offer him your hand in friendship. War is a tactic. The strategy is peace.

Perhaps some of these values apply to women too. I have no idea how to be a woman. My father did not teach me to be a woman. In my family, my wife is in charge of being the woman, and while I like what she does, I have no standard on which to judge her. I do think being a woman is different than being a man, but I intend to say no more on this subject because my father did tell me to avoid annoying the women.

The message my father gave me is not a formula for success in our complex and sophisticated world. It may or it may not work for me; the final score is yet to be tallied. Yet it is a message from one father to one son that has been held in my heart and that I have valued enough to pass on.

I realize that much of this message stands counter to much that is presently held as gospel. I realize that many feel that the woman has as great an economic responsibility as the man. I don't mind women—including my wife—feeling that. I even appreciate it. I just don't feel it.

I know that popular self-actualizing theory does not call for the submergence of self in a greater whole, loyalty above everything, warlike behavior, and truth before self-protective caution. What can I say other than that I have been trained in such theory and practiced such theory, and in the last analysis, I don't believe in it. I use a little of it to salt Charlie's raw-meat doctrine of manhood. I take better care of myself than he did. But I have decided that he provided the meat, and self-actualizing theory is only the salt.

If I had had the courage or the stupidity to talk back to the thespians of the men's conference, I might have said: All fathers teach their sons to be men (as do all mothers teach their daughters to be women). My father did not say out loud any of the values I have presented as his. Some things are too important to be said out loud. It may be that some fathers' model for manhood is so second-rate that their sons do not want to hear it. It may be that some sons think of themselves as so sophisticated that simple messages get ignored as outmoded or not reflecting modern psychological understanding. But don't tell me that your dad didn't teach you anything. As Charlie said: "I have taught you everything I know, and you don't know anything."

Hey, Dad, I'll settle for the nothing you taught me.

SNOW

———————— ✕ ————————

SUPER BOWL SUNDAY IS COMING UP. THIS YEAR THE GAME is to be held at the Hubert H. Humphrey Metrodome in Minneapolis, right across the river from where I live. The weather forecasters and sports reporters are in a tizzy, fearful that hordes of wealthy and important national figures on their first trip here will be greeted with a blast of the famous Minnesota winter. Since I have never lived outside Minnesota, my only way of understanding how others feel about our winters is to hear what our media say. Apparently our winters make people nervous.

I like winter. That is a good thing in an area of the country that has, as my father used to say, nine months of winter and three months of poor sledding. The glory of winter is the snow. Falling gently, it's downright pretty. The drifts change the shape of summer's landscape. And blizzards? In a blizzard I feel a peace that I will never feel in any situation outside of heaven.

The Halloween blizzard of 1991 was a dream fulfilled. It is about twenty degrees—not too cold. A light wind blows. And there is day after day of snow—twenty-nine inches in all. Cars get stuck in the street. Buses no longer run. Ambulances have to be towed to emergencies by fire trucks. Businesses shut down.

I am as happy as I am because I am ready for this. All summer long I roll around in my four-wheel-drive vehicle, grinding gears, accelerating with difficulty, suffering innumerable bounces, jolts, and minor indignities that would not be mine to bear in a sedan of any make. But this Halloween my Isuzu Trooper and I are in our glory. A trip to the movies? The grocery store? Hit a restaurant for breakfast? Kid needs to be picked up? I'm happy to do it! I knock the snow off the windshield, kick the lever into four-wheel drive, and let out the clutch. I feel her dig down through the drift, find purchase, and off we go. I even carry a chain to hook on to the vehicles of the less fortunate when time and inclination direct.

In the corner of my garage sits the snowblower. With two pulls, a cough, a rattle, and a roar, I blast the drifts off of my walk, take out Mort's in honor of his age, hit Barb and Lea's because they are two women and my mom taught me chivalry, and then whop off Jerry's because he is a good neighbor, so why not? Lord, do I feel righteous when I'm tackling a snowstorm.

Then I go inside, stack the cold outdoor clothes by the radiator, light the fire, heat the coffee, get the novel, turn on the stereo, and settle on the davenport with nothing to do because in Minnesota when it gets like this, normal business stops.

I am a worrier. In a sense, I have nothing to worry about. As I have often told myself while worrying, I am in sound shape financially. My consulting business provides an excellent salary, even after Uncle Sam hits me with the self-employment tax. My wife is supportive emotionally and has a good job with salary and benefits on which most families could live well. I have talents. I have friends. My health is fine. My sons are approaching manhood and will make it on their own no matter what I do now. The house is nearly paid for. My cars have three more years on them. My dock fee for next summer is paid. I have adequate work lined up for the next four months and some prospects beyond that.

Anytime someone tells you this many reasons to feel secure, you can be sure that you are listening to a worrier.

People who don't worry don't have a list of reasons why they don't have to worry.

But I don't worry when the snow is coming down, particularly when it's coming down hard. There are things to do. Missions to be accomplished. Everything else is set aside, and the task becomes simply survival. The satisfaction is the discovery that I am surviving very well indeed. And I could survive even better if I were to four-wheel my way down to the liquor store for some whiskey to sip by the fire tonight.

I have learned from winter snowstorms. Anxiety is what happens when the worry machine is working without anything to work on. It's a little like running the snowblower in gear without snow or lifting a boat propeller out of the water with the motor running. Or using four-wheel drive on a dry highway. In order to stop worrying, even in the summertime, I create my own blizzard. Any distant worry can be turned into a present task. These tasks can be fed into the worry machine. They can be accomplished. The machine stops groaning or moaning. The whiskey tastes good, and the bed provides a satisfied rest instead of a sleepless night.

I sit down and list what is bothering me. Then I list the tasks that fit with this worry. Then I put the tasks on the calender in the blank places where I might otherwise just sit around and worry. Then I do them with alacrity. If I'm concerned about publishing the next book, I write a chapter. If I'm feeling pressured about clients I haven't seen, I see them. If I'm worried about finances, I create a spreadsheet and start tracking where I am and where I'm going at the present rate. If I'm anxious about my relationships, I call my friends, maybe even have a party.

I suppose that, like a Minnesota winter, this approach sounds painful. I assure you, it does not hurt. Task after task pours on my head with the calming effect of snow.

Soon I feel my shoulders relax, my stomach quiet down, and my head clear as shovelful by shovelful I work my worries away. What happens when enough has been done so that I am no longer worried? Why, I sit down. Satisfied, I contemplate the clean walks, my wife and son's cars towed to the haven of a snug garage, and the Trooper waiting patiently out front for another challenge.

The long-range forecast calls for snow on Super Bowl Sunday. The media are preparing their apology to visitors from other climates. I am happy. There will be plenty to do. I might even cruise downtown and yank a couple of limousines out of the drifts. They will think me a helpful guy. Little will they know the peace that a blizzard works in my soul.

ON LOSING THE JOB

WE HAD CLEARED THE SLOT BETWEEN RED CLIFF ON THE mainland and Basswood Island on the starboard side and entered the waters beyond the marker buoy when the wind died. A few days earlier Edith and I had hauled the *Laughing Buddha* to the Bayfield area for two weeks in the Apostle Islands, on Lake Superior. We had selected early August because Lake Pepin becomes hot, green, and still during that period and the winds on Lake Superior are more manageable for a little boat. It should have come as no surprise that the wind had died. Though it was normally a windless time of year, we had had several days of decent wind up until now, and the day's forecast had called for no wind at all, or "light and variable" wind, which is what the National Weather Service says when it means "nothing."

Nevertheless, as we left breakfast on Madeline Island the wind had been blowing, and I told Edith that we had a perfect run up to the lighthouse on Raspberry Island, which I wanted to show her. It was just appearing beyond the hills of Oak Island when the wind died. I was very disappointed.

I am a stubborn man. I have been known to sit in a calm for half a day hoping for a wind, indeed seeing almost invisible puffs, some of which actually reach my boat and move it a few feet. That's what I did this day. Edith retired to the cabin and read a book as I struggled to move forward, altering the sail settings to catch a breath of air first off one side, then off the other, a little push from behind, a chance to tack into a head wind. At one time several boats a mile ahead of me caught a nifty wind and accelerated away, but that wind died before it reached me.

Since Edith's reading was being interrupted by my thumping and cursing, from time to time she would emerge from the hatch and suggest that I use the motor. "Not enough gas to make it to Raspberry and back," I would say. Finally she began to suggest that we motor back to Schooner Bay where we could tie up, I could buy a cold beer and some gas, and we could find some shade to sit in. It took a while, but I finally gave up, started the motor, putted back around the corner, slid through the sea gate, and found an empty berth. "Welcome to paradise!" the harbormaster said. He didn't know the half of it. Paradise looks ever so much better when you have been sitting in hell.

Have you ever lost a job?

I have, twice. One of the nice things about being a Roman Catholic priest was that I would never lose my job. Punishment would be to receive a poorer job, but never no job. Shortly after I had joined Honeywell, when our division was experiencing tight times, my colleague, Don, stuck his head in the office to say that the boss wanted to see me. "I think they are letting you go," he said. Then he apologized. "Just kidding," he said. He told me later that he had made the joke because he thought I would know it was a ridiculous idea, that I was as safe as if I were in the church, and he had backed off the joke when he saw my face turn absolutely white with fear. He thought I might faint.

He did not know how safe churches were and how frightened I was of real life or he would not have teased me.

That time I did not lose my job. I eventually left Honeywell on my own steam to enter a tiny consulting firm. Three years later, when the boss set up a meeting with me, I knew what was coming. I had been billing at 50 percent against a standard of 80 percent while he had been billing at about 120 percent. He was tired of carrying me. I resigned at the start of the meeting, thereby putting a good face on things. There were lots of words about it being time for me to go out on my own, but I had no doubt in my mind that I had not made the grade. Thirteen years later Control Data showed me the door. It was a time of economic downturn; others were being let go from our division, and within months the whole division had collapsed, but it was not lost on me that I was the first from my unit to be given the opportunity to practice my skills on the street. It is an ugly feeling.

What I am afraid of when I lose a job is never doing anything deserving of my talents again. When I lose my job, I lose my chance to impact the universe. I fear being tucked away in a pleasant house, living off my wife at a level of comfort many would be pleased to have. I can fill my days reading, walking, and doing the dishes. But I will be out of it.

It makes no difference that I am a lovely boat, that the hull has been designed to glide, the sails shaped for maximum leverage, or even that I am the best boat for the price in the fleet. Pull away my job and the wind goes dead, the joyful bubble of water is silenced at the bow, and the sense of motion, of purpose, is gone. In no wind the boat is no longer valued. It is a hot, frustrating, annoying place. With no job, of what worth am I? Why be thrilled at a sailboat's features if it is only to be tied to the dock?

I would ask those who create the philosophies on which corporations are run to emphasize that the first task of the corporation is to provide people with the opportunity to work. The primary reason for growing a corporation is to provide more jobs. Profit and return to shareholders are means to that end. Even service to customers comes second. When jobs are emphasized, these three goals will be served because if they are not, there will be no jobs. But the goal of making a few people wealthy beyond need will not be served. The leveraged buyouts that create a few rich people at the cost of placing millions of useful workers out of work are not crimes but sins against humanity.

When you are cruising down Lake Pepin on a gentle day, it is considered polite to steer your boat so that you avoid blocking the wind. It is in the nature of boats that big boats always catch up to little boats. You will see them pass on the downwind side, suffering a slight cut in their own speed as they enter the little boat's wind shadow, but avoiding stopping the little boat entirely with theirs. When people tell me they are working sixty-hour weeks, I wish they would cut back to forty and hire an assistant. Why hog the work? Why get rid of the slightly less capable worker in favor of keeping the slightly more capable during a downturn? Why not go to a thirty-two-hour week? There is no more tragic sight to me than a person without useful work. We should go to great lengths to avoid emptying the hands of even one craftsperson.

We sailboaters are obsessed with wind. I walk out of an office building and check the flags despite the fact that whether they are stiff or limp my car will travel just fine on the freeway. The speed and direction of the wind register on me even when I am weeks and miles away from my sailboat. "Nice day," the receptionist says. "Darn right," I say. "Wind due south at eighteen. Beam reach up and down Pepin. Super day!"

We need to look at every move for its impact on jobs the way I look at every turn of the wind for its impact on sailing. "Like hell you will drop out of advanced math," the father says to his child. "You need a job someday, and you won't get one without knowing math." The union votes not to take a pay raise and to avoid overtime so a few more people can experience the dignity of a paycheck. The executive skips his bonus so that others may be employed.

I wake up this morning to a gray spring day. There is no wind out there. I am in the Cities, not down at the lake, so I am not much frustrated by the fact that it is a poor day to sail. Today I have work. There is work for the rest of this month and prospects for the rest of the year. It feels good. The wind blows!

RULES FOR FINDING YOURSELF

NOW THAT I AM NEARING THE CLOSE OF MY FIFTY-SEVENTH year, I do believe that I am beginning to know who I am. The course could have been traversed ever so much more quickly if I had known some rules for finding myself, but the rules have only become clear to me during the search. I pass them on to you so that you need not waste time searching in unproductive closets and so that you might more quickly recognize clues when they are handed to you and not spurn them, as I have, until the tenth time the universe placed them under my nose.

Do not try to be unique. You already are unique. Aren't we all? If you try to be different from other people, you may be pouring untold energy into maintaining characteristics ill-suited for you. That is what teenagers do. Allow them that. They do not know that they can be different than their parents, so they work very hard at contradicting their parents' values, customs, dress, and interests. When they discover they can succeed at being different, most of them relax and become very much like their parents. I assume you are not a teenager. An easier road is open to you.

Take tests. Take tests, starting with the written kind: Myers-Briggs Type Indicator, Strong-Campbell, DISC, or even the *Reader's Digest* superspecials. Although they have various degrees of validity, none of them are real predictors of anything. But each of them gives another handle on who that creature is that you call you.

Take other kinds of tests, too. Pick up challenges to do

something different. Climb a mountain, camp in the woods, read *War and Peace*. Indeed, you may hate doing it as much as you thought you would, and you may be as poor at it as you predicted, and you may never want to do it again. But every test teaches you something new about yourself.

Listen to your friends. For a long time I regularly wrote a rather pedantic newsletter. One day I wrote from the heart and did not stop, because I was having fun. When I published what I thought were nearly inappropriate thoughts, my friends raved on about how moving and delightful they found that issue. For the next two years the balance in my writing moved from the head to the heart as I listened to the fluctuations in the applause meter. Look for what others delight in. Allow them to illuminate your talents with the glow of their approval.

Listen to those who reject you. I hate being rejected. I feel rejection to the core of my being. I think that in turning me away, others are saying that I am a worthless human being. I know they are wrong. I hate them for their stupidity. I plan revenge. I vow that when my day comes, I will reject them. I allow myself all of these feelings. I am the kind of person who feels like that. It's too bad, but it's true.

On good days, however, I learn from my moments of rejection. Whoever rejected me did not intend to reject me as a whole human being. They saw some characteristics that they didn't like or that didn't fit what they wanted, and it was those characteristics that they rejected. What are they? You may learn something about who you are from what those who reject you see. Although serious reflection about why you were on the discard list may reveal some weaknesses, this need not be a completely negative learning experience.

A weakness usually is another way of describing a corresponding strength. "If they don't want me because I am not careful enough, I'm probably a risk taker, and others in other situations will want me for the very reason I was rejected in this situation." Don't be quick to reform yourself to please those who don't like you. You may ruin the real you. Self-acceptance usually beats reformation as a change strategy anyway. When I am disgusted with my weight, I seem to keep gaining it. When I accept it as a tolerable weakness, often I begin the successful diet.

Allow yourself empty time. Constantly running around obscures the inner self. The first four rules are about learning from the ricochets of life. This one is about withdrawing and finding out who you are when you are not being tested and judged. Consider slowing down enough to reflect on what happens inside and who dwells there. Learn to meditate, maybe even pray. At least take a long and gentle walk until the storm in your head works itself free through your feet and allows you to sort out the essential facts of who is walking here.

The search for that true and essential self is never over if you are a true searcher. Everything you do, including the searching itself, adds to who you are. Indeed, I wonder if those who have found themselves in some final way have not really simply chosen to limit the definition of who they are to a few simple and manageable features, ignoring the rest. Year after year I am astonished to discover what I've been keeping under the wraps of this body I've been wearing for nearly six decades.

I was speaking to a friend of mine about death. He was not afraid of the possibility, only sad that in his sixty-fifth year he had nearly become the human being he was intended to be. It seemed a waste to not let the product hang around a few decades now that it was nearly complete.

The search for self is a worthy project. The sooner that self is mostly found, the sooner it can be enjoyed.

THE RUDDER

I HAD BEEN DOWN ON PEPIN FOR A FEW DAYS, SOMETIMES sailing alone, sometimes with friends. The day before, I had slashed my way uplake in twenty knots of wind all the way to Frontenac. The *Buddha* had behaved like a champ. This Sunday morning I got my act together to go home and then waited to give a ride to a couple I did not know. They owned the seventeen-foot version of my boat, were thinking of moving up to the twenty-three-foot model, and wanted to see how the bigger boat sailed.

We went out in about twelve knots of wind. We were flying the largest sails and making top speed with a couple of three-mile tacks behind us when the man said he had heard a cracking sound. I crawled down the swim ladder to find that the rudder seemed bent. But that didn't seem possible. We took down the front sail, turned downwind toward home, and then, just to be sure, I grounded the boat on a beach and crawled off to take a look. I could bend the rudder with my foot! We pushed off and started back, with the wife on the tiller. After we'd gone a quarter mile, I asked her to point the nose down, and she said, "I think it's gone."

Her husband leaned over the back of the boat. "Shark got it," he said.

The top quarter of the rudder waved in the air. The bottom three quarters had disappeared into the lake.

Using the motor for power and control, we got the sails down and brought her home. I have never driven a sailboat without a rudder. It isn't easy. The motor on this boat is an outboard, so it can be turned, but even so, the *Buddha*, which normally responds to a flick of the wrist, fought my every move. Our trip into the slip was less a landing than a barely controlled collision with the dock.

If you were to look at the rudder whole, it would not be clear why it has such effect. Compared to twenty-three feet of boat and to its heavy keel, the rudder is only a light three-by-two-foot blade. Yet without the rudder the boat not only won't turn on command, she won't even go straight. If I had left her under sail, we would have spent our day facing the wind, bobbing slowly up and down. The rudder is a small but vital component of the boat's design.

I sometimes wonder where the rudder is on a human being. In consulting to corporations, I have met many people floating rudderless, bow to the wind. "Sure, boss," they say, and whichever way the boss blows, their sterns swing around, neatly pointing back into the wind, bobbing in passive delight, making no motion forward, sideways, or back. "No rudder," I say. But what do I mean?

My hunch is that the rudder in a person is located slightly below the heart, perhaps a quarter inch above the solar plexus. It's name is Desire, or Self-Direction, or Personal Ambition. It is that part of people that aims them at their own goals, directs them toward their own vision, demands that they do what needs to be done to fulfill their own dreams.

Indeed, sometimes management finds people with rudders annoying. They argue back. They want to do things their way. Often they pursue their own interests besides, as well as, or instead of the corporation's. But they do move. The rudderless do not.

My rudder did not break in a day. Two months before this incident, my friend Mary Lou and I were sailing, she on the tiller, me on the sheets, into three-foot waves. The *Buddha* charged over the waves with speed and power and had just settled into a trough when we felt a solid thud. Mary Lou felt it more than I did. The shock came up the tiller into her hand. "Maybe we sat on a log?" I said. But we saw nothing and we were still sailing, so we pressed on. Later, when I examined the broken rudder, I could see the crack that was started that day and finally gave out months after that.

I think everybody is born with desire. The baby cries in desire for the nipple. The child shouts for his candy bar. The teenager acts up to gain recognition. The student struggles for certification. The corporate employee walks in the door eager to begin a successful career. We don't sail exactly where the wind intends. Too often, instead of offering gentle advice for those bearing far off the hoped-for course, or tolerance for those bearing off only a few degrees, somebody—mother, teacher, or boss—decides to throw a log in our way, give us a shock, shape us up, drive us to the intended course.

There are many kinds of logs: "Daddy is busy." "Cut your hair right or you can move out." "I don't care if Joyce Kilmer mixed his metaphors. You don't pass my class if you mix yours." "If you hope to succeed around here, little lady, you better remember that he who has the gold, rules." The boat comes around for now. But one day its battered rudder breaks. The boat sails no more. It bobs gently in the breeze, docile and meek. Good for little, perhaps good for nothing.

Today the *Laughing Buddha* sits tamely in her slip, awaiting the arrival of a new rudder from her birthplace in Florida. God or some mortal fool pushed a log into the lake. Which seems to me, generally speaking, a bad idea.

LEISURE TIME

Some of you are too young to know this, and some of you have forgotten it. So let me tell you about it. In 1965 there was a spate of books and articles discussing how we were to use our leisure time. The sociologists and the psychologists were worried about us. Technological indicators revealed that the work week would soon be shortened by at least several hours. Workers would have their work cut in half by computers and robots. The homebound mother would now have her freedom, with technology cooking the meals and doing the wash. We were going to have time on our hands and needed help dealing with it.

It is no wonder that those of my generation have forgotten these predictions as they lug full briefcases home from work every evening and spend some of Saturday at the office. It is no wonder that thirty-year-old mothers, who have indeed been freed from the kitchen, only to find themselves chained to the desk, can't believe that such books were ever written.

So what happened on the way to paradise?

Some other people liked what we had and decided to wrestle with us for their piece of what was in the sixties an American pie. They were the Japanese, most prominently, but also the Koreans, the Yugoslavians, certainly the Germans, the Taiwanese—you name them. They decided that they would hustle our markets, take advantage of our complacency, and eat from our table. As a matter of fact, the Japanese now own a fair chunk of our table, as do the British and the Dutch.

If there is one thing we Americans are good at, it is gearing up for a fight. We are meeting global competition head-on, trying to match our rivals punch for punch and hustle for hustle. Which leaves us all in a funny place. They want to have what we had. But we no longer have it. We have less disposable income than we did in the fifties and less time to dispose of it precisely because we are hustling to be like them.

So when somebody says to me that if we don't do things the way the Japanese do them, they will own us, I say, let them own us. I don't want to live like the Japanese do. Heck, the Japanese don't want to live like the Japanese do. They want to live like we used to.

Could we take an international time out from this race, perhaps sponsored by the United Nations? Let's try to remember where we were going when we all got caught up in this marathon. If we could slow down a little, I've got some good books left over from the sixties on the use of leisure that I would like to read sometime.

GET A WIFE

NEARLY TEN YEARS AGO MY WIFE AND I TOOK ADVANTAGE of an opportunity presented by the training organization to which I belonged to attend a course for two-career couples on problems they face. Since Edith and I both worked for the corporation, I as a corporate guru for training and she as a whirling dervish of marketing administration, and since both of us were raising two grade-school boys, the course seemed made for us.

As we talked through the difficulties we faced as two-career couples, I heard many familiar stories from the other people in the class: of leaving an eleven-year-old with a fever home alone on the day you're scheduled to make a big presentation; of getting midday phone calls inquiring why your child is not in school when you thought he was, and after some frantic phone calls it turns out that he is, but that somebody put a check in the wrong place on the attendance sheet; of attending a child's talent show while wondering if your boss really needed the report you didn't quite have time to finish; of watching a blizzard through office windows unsure if the kids remembered their house keys when they went to school.

I think that couples without children don't have quite the difficulty juggling two careers that couples with children experience. Of the twelve couples in this class, all had children, and almost all the difficulties presented had to do with children. Couples without children may resent the fact that Edith and I sometimes forget they're married, but chauvinistic as our perspective is, that husband will survive his wife's business trip to the West Coast without a sitter, even if he misses her terribly. Their child would not.

Edith and I experience only a glimmer of the pain facing the single parent. It is hard for me to imagine how any one person alone pulls off the myriad responsibilities that Edith and I share, and does it without having another person to argue with about what must be done.

What I learned in that class was: "To get to the top in business, have children, and be moderately happy, you need a wife." "Wife" in this instance has to do not with gender, but with a role; it is a person whose sole function is to keep you rolling.

I heard that some corporation or other has passed a rule that meetings can't be held after three in the afternoon so that those with family responsibilities are free to leave when they must. If you are upward bound in that corporation, I'd advise you to experience no peace of mind over that rule. So nobody will call a meeting. But five people will get together at six that night and they will make a decision that you will be out of unless you decide to skip picking up the kid at the standard time. Hey, they aren't out to get you, they're just getting the job done. You can't be there, and they forgive you, but they write you off. That's life.

I came to this conclusion in the two-career-couple class. While nobody talked about it or even said it aloud until this class, the word on all of us was that our families came first and the corporation a distant second. That was the first time I told myself I was going nowhere—"nowhere" at least as defined by the corporate value system in which "somewhere" is up the ladder.

And that is where I have gone. I am a small-time consultant after being a small-time bureaucrat. I don't generate nearly the income some of my friends generate as consultants. That is because I only have half a wife. And my wife is not going to the top of her business, because she has only half a wife—me.

Without wholehearted dedication a business will not thrive, a career will advance only so far. To have that wholehearted dedication and a family requires a support person willing to sacrifice everything and anything to keep the earner rolling, gaining on the competition. The shirts must be ironed, the children coiffed, the furnace fixed, and the groceries bought and cooked so that the earner can put on the shirt, eat the breakfast, kiss the children, and enter the lists ready to charge through the tourney until all others have fallen, returning home only when needing to, not when home needs him or her, because it doesn't.

I like doing it my way. My consulting business does not excel, but it does all right, and I do appreciate knowing that if it failed completely, Edith's paycheck and benefits will carry us nicely. I enjoy attending the hockey games, the band concerts, and even the conferences with teachers. As I say to Edith, "I'm the highest-paid househusband in town!" Winning at business is one way to do it. My way is another. But if you don't want to get hung up in the middle, neither coming out on top in business nor experiencing some success in all life's roles, I suggest accepting this rule as a law of nature: "If you haven't got a wife, be content with a lower spot on the hill. If you want to come out on top of the heap, get a wife!"

OUR CEO WHO ART ON
THE TOP FLOOR

I BELONG TO A SMALL GROUP OF PEOPLE EXPLORING SPIRI-
tuality together. All of us were brought up as Christians,
but of twelve people, only four of us presently practice
Christianity. We started our discussions a year or so ago
at the Episcopal House of Prayer on the grounds of the
Benedictine Abbey of St. John's in central Minnesota.
As I negotiated our yearly retreat, I found out that the
Episcopal church refers to us as "the business group,"
which charms me not a little since this motley collec-
tion of believers and nonbelievers outsearches any
"church group" I have sat with up there.

This group held a meeting last Sunday, which I could
not attend but which I heard about later. After more than
a year we are welcoming a new member, someone who is
becoming more closely attached to one of the group's
founders. Since he is Jewish, one member of our group, in
an attempt to make him feel comfortable, told him that
religion is just an accent and has little to do with the
basic spiritual message of our gatherings. I thought that
was a kind act, even if he was nearly totally wrong.

Religion is not an accent. Religion is a language.

Concepts are not only communicated by the language,
they are formed by it. As one author put it, she refuses to
use the American spelling for *gray* when she writes about
England because the color she is talking about is the grey
that occurs in England, and that can only be indicated by
the British spelling.

I recently saw a television commercial praising the Lincoln over the Mercedes. Unfortunately for Ford, their advertising people, in an effort to appear quite scientific, had a real German scientist announce the results of the expensive test that had been conducted. The scientist stated that *this* Lincoln had beaten *this* Mercedes in *this* test, implying that some other Lincoln in some other test might well be trounced by some other Mercedes—which is the hard fact. Ford should have realized that anyone who has spoken German from birth picks articles with care. German is a language punitive to sloppy thinkers. That is why it is the language of science.

French used to be the language of diplomacy. At the college I went to, when you ruined another man's day by destroying him on the athletic field, you murmured, "*C'est la guerre,*" which seemed to soothe the opponent's afflictions. The literal translation, "That's war," probably would not have as comforting an effect. And the intended translation, "Tough shit," probably would have provoked further combat. It is difficult to be nasty in the fluid language of France, although the French must be given credit for frequently succeeding at it.

Religion is a language. It defines the reality it conveys. So what happens to a group of people who from childhood have been taught to pray to "our Father, who art in heaven"? Do they not learn to expect that up there somewhere there are persons capable of governing their world? As they enter corporate life, they learn, that on the top floor there is a CEO who is in charge of making everything right.

Have you noticed the number of corporations whose officers choose the top floor for their offices? Why, if not to imitate the father in heaven, would someone choose to ride an elevator for twenty-eight floors when he could walk in and sit on the first floor?

Have you noticed the reverence with which many corporate employees refer to the CEO? IDS, a very successful division of American Express in the days of Harvey Golub, had employees who would pause before mentioning his name with the deference deserved by Yahweh. Even those who hate the CEO tend to hate him for being a poor god, not for being a poor human. This was the case with everybody who told me that Jim Renier was screwing up Honeywell. How can one man screw up, or fix, or do anything significant to a corporation that large without the complicity of thousands of others? People whose religious language has trained them to believe in a father in heaven expect an all-knowing and all-powerful leader on the top floor.

I have consulted to two CEOs who were constitutionally incapable of taking on the role. Both of them not only were convinced they were human but acted on a human scale. (Most of the CEOs I have worked for knew they were human but decided that they had better play the game the way the rules are set.) Both of the more modest CEOs provoked consternation among the troops. One of them described his strategy this way: "I have studied our market. I see potential for digging up gold in a number of areas. You I have put in charge of one of these areas with money and people to mine it. If there is no gold there, I have made a mistake and I will not fault you. If there is gold there, it is your job to dig it up profitably. If you need suggestions or help from me, I am here."

Now that seemed clear to me, but more of his troops than I can count said, "What did he say? What does he want?" God had failed to speak from Sinai. Another human had just pointed to a job and said, Do it anyway, you know how, because I don't know how to do it better than you do, and by the way, I'm not even sure it can be done. This is very disappointing to eyes and ears chronically aimed heavenward.

Most people will say that religion has no connection with business. Nonsense! Religion is one of our first languages, and it shapes everything else we do. I sat at a table with an executive team of ten people, and on a dare I correctly named the religious backgrounds of each person, despite the fact they had discussed only business and never religion. (Don't ask me to try this again. I know I was lucky, and a botched second try would ruin the story.)

For this reason, I want to amend the Lord's prayer: The Our Father makes for poor business. Christianity, to which I adhere with ardor, has its negative features, one of which is that it leaves too many people looking to the upper floors for divine guidance. The most likely result of this is a crick in the neck.

LOVE AND FORGIVENESS

DAD CAME BACK FROM THE GAS COMPANY THAT DAY really angry. "Damn fool says we're supposed to love people." And then, with an irritated sideways glance, "You don't know this Larry Wilson guy, do you?" I admitted that I knew him slightly. Charlie went on. The company had hired Larry to conduct a one-day session with some of the employees, and Larry had talked about the importance of love for the success of a company. Charlie and the rest of the gas-company gang had not liked it much.

I tried defending Larry a little, assuring Dad that the operative word was not "nuts." "Eccentric" might be applicable, and certainly "unique" (this was 1969), but nonetheless, Larry had something valuable to say. I lost the argument, not by force of intellect but by force of will.

In the long run Larry has won out. He built a corporation while peddling his concepts and now sits down in New Mexico in the midst of a retreat center that, among other things, allows people to explore the role of love in business. Others have taken up the cry under various formats. And I, Charlie's son, am unfaithful to the old man in this. I'm sticking with Larry. Love has a place in business.

There are four levels of love. The first level is to love that which pleases. Business is good at that. I particularly notice this when someone new is hired into the executive ranks. She is super, extraordinary, obviously a great performer and ever so much better than the old director, who had failing upon failings. I don't give much credit to a business that loves what it finds pleasing. What else would any sane person do?

The second level of love is to forgive the failings of those we love. Businesses that reach this level work ever so much more effectively than those that don't. A group of my colleagues had an enormous laugh when I suggested that it would be more effective if instead of appraising employees, worrying about their weak points, and trying to place them accurately across the salary curve based on the subtleties of their performance, they fire the 2 percent who are really losers, promote the 2 percent who are really winners, and tell the rest that they are average, that if they will buckle down to work, they will do just fine because with regularity this corporation will give average increases and average promotions to the majority of its employees.

I hadn't planned to be funny. I had not even planned to be insightful. Most people are average. That is the definition of average: "most people." So why worry about it? Forgive them for being average. If they please you enough that you love them enough to hire them into the corporation and do not want to fire them, forgive them their flaws, peccadilloes, and imperfections. It's cheaper. It improves motivation and leaves everybody feeling much cleaner.

A third level of love is to forgive first, and then love. We humans have such high ideals, especially for other people. We have this image of the ideal boss, who is kind, strict, wise, shrewd, caring, supportive, and mentoring. Any boss fails when compared to this image. So most of us waste untold energies complaining because the boss is less than a paragon—as is the secretary, as are colleagues. Where does this image of the ideal come from? I don't know. I once heard it suggested that a corporation close its college recruiting division in the personnel department and hire only people who have worked for someone else before. Then they will know that it is not this corporation that is filled with ignorance and waste, but every corporation. It is the human condition.

If we can accept the fact that the company we are in is inefficient and prodigal, and forgive it for being what it is, then we can love it, and instead of complaining about it, we can improve it, which will without doubt improve the bottom line.

I once complained to a friend of mine that nobody ever called me. I always called my friends, took them out to breakfast, and inquired about their well-being, and I was getting irritated at their lack of proactiveness. "John," he said in the tone of the wise guru, "there are two kinds of people, callers and callees. Which are you?"

Without hesitation I responded, "A caller."

"Then quit bitching about it. You belong to an exclusive set. There are not many like you. Go find a telephone and start calling." And forgive the callees for not being proactive.

There is a fourth level of love. It starts from this willingness to forgive the universe for being the universe, but drops into something even deeper. Those who have reported it to me tell me that when experiencing this level of love, the sense of self is lost and there is a feeling of being a part of the whole instead of an individual acting against or with others. For some reason, they say, while feeling that loss of individuality they felt more important and effective, not less so. They felt no need to compete or succeed, but they felt that whatever they did was play, rich in color, a reward in itself.

I have known of this phenomenon for some time. I always assumed that this was a religious sensation not of interest to the business community—until I heard this story:

One of the major consulting firms was trying its psychological theory in corporations in other countries to see if its model of personality types was culturally determined or would work universally. To test the model they would sit in business meetings, categorize the people in the meeting, then check out the categories by testing the individual after the meeting. For them to succeed in developing a cross-cultural model, every person they met should be describable according to their system. Their theory worked just fine everywhere, even in India—with an occasional exception. Those exceptions were disturbing.

Sometimes in meetings a person from the company would sit in who according to his job title had no reason to be there. This person seldom spoke, but when he was invited to the meeting, there was usually a useful outcome. The researchers inquired why this person was there; what was his role? The answer was that he was a holy man, and in his presence everything went better, so in critical situations he was asked to just *be* there.

So perhaps business has a use for the fourth level of love, but let me go no further, for I am sure my father would not approve.

A SMALL GOSPEL

To RUN A GREAT BUSINESS, YOU MUST UNDERSTAND THE nature of gospels. To be a great businessperson, you have to have a gospel. Here is what you must understand:

All gospels are small. Centuries ago a Jewish peasant said that you should love God and your neighbor. It's not a long sentence, but the rest of Christianity is only commentary on this text. The Buddha said to put aside desire. The temples and their statues are but accretions on this pearl. The Lakota name their god, and everything else is an unnecessary explication, for their god's name is "The Togetherness of All Things." What's left to be said?

All gospels dictate an attitude. One small set of words regulating one key attitude will take the place of a twenty-volume compendium of law. If the attitude is there, the correct behavior will follow. This is what Paul meant when he wrote that the law was given to us because of the hardness of our hearts. We did not want to change our attitude, so we had to be controlled by law.

This is why some corporations have policies to cover everything. No one has thought out the basic attitude of the corporation or has thought to communicate it. Frequently the basic attitude would be embarrassing to put into words. Nobody wants to say that their gospel is "Greed is good."

Gospels are promulgated by behavior. They are not spread by word, but by actions. Jesus was not the only person— and certainly not the only Jew—to announce the gospel of love. He acted it out to the hilt. Every Native American holy person who I have known says with his or her simplest action that all things are together. Analyze the way she drinks her coffee and see that no other conclusion is possible.

Nobody cares that the CEO says that quality is first, but they notice that the only number he ever comments on is revenue. People are always in search of their corporation's gospel, and they read it not in the words of the leadership but in its behavior.

Unless the core survives, all additions to the basic gospel are hollow. Christianity has had to be continually called back to the simple notion that God is love. When it has become overly concerned with the trappings and forgetful of the core, it has often become rotten in its very heart. Reformers have always arrived bearing a very simple message, the small gospel, the one stated at the beginning of the institution they hope to reform.

All people are gospel seekers. At some level in our consciousness, all of us are aware that our lives are precious and should not be cast away in a purposeless endeavor. I have met few people unwilling to respond to a call that touches the heart.

There are businesspeople who *do* understand the nature of a gospel. Sam Walton, the founder of Wal-Mart, understood and had his own. Every fiber of his being radiated the gospel of cost-effective service. He spent little on himself and was of service to his own employees. After Sam made his genial way through the store, expressing enthusiastic interest in what the staff was doing, how could any employee not greet a customer with care and solicitude? Wal-Mart has all the stuff other businesses have: computers, automated checkout, management systems, buyers, clerks. And all the other retail outlets have what Wal-Mart has—except for Sam Walton and his gospel. And now Sam's ghost, which is very much alive. It makes a difference.

I was very surprised to discover that most brokerage firms have no way of knowing how much money they are making for their customers. I found it out when the company to which I was consulting began a program to judge their brokers not on how much they make in commissions, the standard industry measure, but on how well their clients do financially, based on their brokers' advice.

Just before the program was started, I met one of the leading brokers in the firm, a man whose commission level was always in the top ten and who was manager of the most profitable branch. I asked him his secret. "I make money for my customers," he said.

"How much?" I asked, knowing that he couldn't know the answer. He gave me the average return on investment he had helped his clients earn for each of the last five years. In case I didn't get that, he took me through it a second time using the average investment per customer for each year and the average dollar amount earned. I stopped him as he began to work his way through the difference between those who had invested more than a certain amount and those who had invested less.

"How do you know that? I asked. "There is no system in place to calculate that data."

He looked at me with disgust. "How could I not know it? Everybody in my branch knows how much money they make for their customers. I don't care how they find it out. Get a computer program. Use a calculator. Buy a pencil. But know whether or not you are doing people any good."

There was his gospel: "Make money for your customers." Policy manuals, dress codes, statements of ethics, and paper-flow systems were just somewhat helpful add-ons. Every broker in his office knew the name of the game, not because he said it so often, although he would say it, but because he acted it out so vigorously.

Ed Deming, the grandfather of both Japanese and

American quality, said that most problems are caused by the system. Companies that have organized around that gospel have watched costs go down and quality and production go up. Sure, there are a million things to learn after you buy Deming's gospel, statistics being a lot of them, but once you have had the attitude shift demanded by the gospel, the rest of it falls into place readily.

More than one corporation has taught its people statistics to no avail. Some, I suspect, have even won the Baldrige Award by energetically going through the motions without shifting to the basic gospel. It should be no surprise. After all, Confirmation ceremonies do not produce Christians, Bar Mitzvahs do not produce devout Jews, and vision quests do not produce holy people.

The realignment must occur in the middle of the gut.

My experience is that business has little respect for religion. This is not unreasonable; there is a lot about religion that deserves disrespect. But I think it a mistake not to understand the workings of a gospel, for great businesses always are built around one. Marketing strategies, business plans, computer models, inventory levels, and skill training are all good and useful endeavors. But without a central gospel they are as empty as the Christianity of the Inquisition.

Business leaders might prefer to leave religion to those in ministry, but if you are unwilling to capture your people's hearts with a gospel deserving their dedication, you have captured nothing. You are governing nothing. You are leading nowhere. And if you live in a corporation that has no gospel, you are being denied the opportunity of consecrating your time with purpose.

VACATION

———⋈———

I BACKED THE *LAUGHING BUDDHA* OUT OF HER SLIP. I LET her slide until she was close to the two-master across the way. Then I shifted to forward, gunned the Johnson, twisted the rudder hard starboard, rehooked the lifeline as she gathered way, turned her to port, and eased the motor as she settled into her one-knot promenade down the harbor. There are twenty-seven boats resting in their slips this Wednesday morning. She slowly parades by them, displaying on her stubby bow a one-foot-tall bronze Buddha balancing on one foot, his arm lifted to the blue-ing sky, his face creased with glee. There are no humans around to see us, but the boats stir slightly against their tethers as we pass, moved with desire to join us in the wind.

We pass *Friendship*, whose owner rides her in any weather; *Sotto Voce*, "In the quiet voice"—what a name for a sailboat; *Bataleur*, Mike's tumbling African eagle. Then *Alida*, the home of the sailing training company Women in the Wind, a boat on which shouting is not allowed; and *Wassergeist*, "the water spirit." Twenty-seventh in the row is *Wu Wei*, which means "the flow and motion of the universe," whose keel Ross dips in salt water for a month every year. As the last in the line she is a fitting signal to me to throw the tiller over, turn to starboard, and head out the gate, from the calm into a light chop. I motor up to half-speed, the autopilot set to ten degrees off the wind. First I set the main halyard on the winch, pull and pull as the mainsail rises two turns, then I tighten her and clamp her off. With another twenty degrees off the wind, I kill and lift the motor. It grows quiet and I raise the genoa and sheet her home as we heel, turn off the autopilot, take the tiller, and adjust to the precisely needed angle of wind. The *Buddha* surges ahead, waves slapping and spraying from her bow, the statue on the bowsprit and the helms-man in the cockpit standing with bellies protruding, their smiles identical.

The waves, the wind, and my concentration wash away my cares, blow away my weariness, empty my mind of the daily turmoil of making a living. I had a boss once who never let people take one day of vacation. "At least a week," he would say, "preferably two. Your spirit needs it. Do the company a favor and go away."

On the Monday after these five splashing days I put the suit back on. My brown face, recently only seen pro-truding from a T-shirt in the misty shower mirror of the Pepin harbor, looks strange now supported by a red tie. "Why am I here? Why am I not there?"

I went to my meeting, mechanically said, "Nice to see you," and was surprised to realize that for the first time in months I meant it. What had washed my colleagues so sparkling clean? I was the guy on the water.

SPIRITUALITY

IT SEEMS THAT THE DAY OF OPENLY DISCUSSING SPIRITUAL-
ity in the workplace is about to arrive. My professional
organization here in Minnesota sponsors a small group
dedicated to that purpose. I must admit that it is poorly
attended and struggles for constant membership in a way
that the Braintrainers or Technical Trainers do not.

I am afraid that for many people the word *spiritual*
rings up connotations more repugnant than attractive.
Spiritual and *profitable* seem antithetical. They should not
be, and are not in reality. The Latin word *spiritus* means
"breath." I define a spiritual person as one who is con-
scious, aware of the special breath of life in all creation,
particularly in humans and certainly in oneself, and acts
accordingly.

As the breath originates in the belly, so the spiritual
person is well grounded in the body, its needs and desires.
The spiritual person sweats, stinks, swears, and does other
things that putting in print would be breaking a taboo.
The spiritual is not the realm of the effete. The spirit is
not separate from the material. It expresses itself in paintings, sonnets, healing, cathedrals, data bases, books,
songs, slag heaps, skyscrapers, wheat fields, and manure
piles. In other words, work is the expression of the spirit.
Benedict, the founder of monasticism, said that to work is
to pray and insisted that his monks have work.

The spirit seeks a workplace. For some that workplace
is the home and the work is the shaping of children. For
others the workplace is the loft, the factory, or the uni-

versity, and the work is the shaping of paintings, printed circuit boards, or minds. The workplace need not be a foreign land to which the spirit is timidly drawn for a paycheck. The workplace is the natural home of the spirit.

The spiritual person entering the workplace asks questions such as these: Is this work worthy of the human spirit? Is this the work that expresses my spirit? Am I respectful of the spirit within my fellow workers? Do I assent to and assist their call? Is this place beautiful enough to be worthy of the presence of the human spirit? Do I make my work a worthy expression of my spirit?

So many workplaces are so stifling because people cannot find a way to breathe their spirituality into work. Without the spirit, there is not life, only motion, and sometimes not even that. The major block to expressing spirituality is the mistaken belief that it must be expressed in the dictums of a particular religion. People think that if they cannot say "Jesus saves" or cannot preface their actions with a lengthy dissertation on their renunciation of their parents' god, they cannot express their spirituality. Quite the contrary is true. Those who pay attention to the questions in the paragraph above will automatically and without fanfare express their spirituality, easily, freely, and with no questions asked. They will choose work well. They will support colleagues. They will seek quality. They will do good work.

Those who object by saying that these results can be achieved without a sense of spirituality miss my point. I am not seeking these results in themselves. I already believe in the spirit and see these as ways the spirit expresses itself. In my hierarchy of being, the spirit does not exist as the servant of the workplace; rather the workplace exists as the playground of the spirit.

Nothing could be worse than to emphasize spirituality in order to improve productivity. As T. S. Eliot had his bishop say in *Murder in the Cathedral*, "It is the greatest treason, to do the right thing for the wrong reason." It can't work. By putting spirituality in service of productivity, one emphasizes productivity, not spirituality, and therefore neither will be enhanced.

Spirituality is like gravity. It must be taken into account because it is there. Ignore it and you are ignoring the most central fact of any human situation. The Hindus greet each other by bowing with folded hands against the breastbone. This miniceremony means: "I salute the divinity within you."

No workplace can be truly alive until we see the divinity within one another, until we experience behind the breastbone the breath of life, until we insist that our work will not be the humdrum product of a sleeping spirit but a glorious monument to who we really are.

GLADIATORS

I AM TRYING TO RAISE GENTLEMEN, MEN OF SENSITIVITY, TO enter the world of life and work.

Dave's mistake came from too much practice. In practice the instructor gives the signal to start and the combatants are expected to make sure the other guy is ready before beginning. This was a Tae Kwon Do tournament. The referee signaled the start, and the other black belt leaped at Dave, connecting with a kick to the teeth while Dave was waiting for the tournament to begin. The rest of the match was called even by the referee. Dave bounced back from that first staggering blow and fought well and hard. He lost by one kick to the teeth.

After that match I found him in the lavatory washing blood from his lips and gently adjusting some wobbly front teeth. I suggested that we had had enough and it was time to go home. He told me that he still had a shot at second place and that the combination of his braces and his mouth guard would keep his teeth as secure in the gymnasium as it would in the truck riding home. He went back and won second place. The trophy is on the mantel.

The stands at the hockey arena in Princeton start at the door and run two-thirds of the way down one side only. I passed with a wave the little group of Highland-Central parents who had made the sixty-mile drive on this dark and snowy night, and I sat at the red line, blissfully uncaring that I was in the middle of the St. Peter parents and fans—uncaring that is, until the game started.

Before the puck was dropped, their section of the stands began to rumble with calls for blood. I have had some experience with this kind of atmosphere, and I know that this is the way the trouble starts. Seldom does it start on the ice. It starts in the stands, but then the high school kids become so inflamed by the shouts of their parents and friends that they begin to turn the game into war.

This is what the St. Peter team was doing now. The checks were frequent and the hits unnecessarily hard. Intimidation continued after the play. Their captain, after a whistle, tried to bully Ben by skating through him, forcing him to step aside. Ben didn't see him coming until the last second, and then, instead of avoiding him, he stiffened his blocky weight lifter's body and with a shrug deposited him on the ice. The crowd screamed in rage. The referee gave Ben a lecture on standing where he was standing. The St. Peter captain vowed his revenge. He tried to take it later in the period, and it cost him a dislocated shoulder. This did not improve the mood in the stands.

I decided between the first and second periods that although I might have poorer visibility, I would be safer if I joined the Highland-Central parents down in the corner of the rink. Between the second and the third periods I caught Ben just as he was reentering the rink to tell him I would have to leave right at the end of the game for a meeting over in St. Cloud. He was massive in his body armor, his steady eyes gazing through the face-mask slits, his hands folded calmly on the top of his stick, as if he were about to step from the kitchen to the living room rather than onto the ice with the St. Peter parents demanding his head and their children attempting to provide it for them.

I am trying to raise gentlemen, men who love and care for others, who are sensitive to feelings and who will make business and the world a better place by their very presence. Hockey and Tae Kwon Do are all part of the process. And if it had been given to me to raise daughters, I would hope to find them playing soccer, volleyball, or basketball on their road to becoming ladies.

I want my children to be gentle, but this world is not always gentle. The parents of St. Peter will be met again in the promotion-hungry colleague willing to do anything for that next raise, who strikes you without compassion. There comes a time when you must hit your challenger so hard that crossing you will never occur to him again. You must spit the blood out, tongue the teeth back into place, and give your rivals precisely the fight they seem to want, and perhaps a little more.

Macalester College being only a couple blocks away, I slipped into the stands to watch the women's soccer game. After suffering a particularly vicious crash a player was assisted into the dressing room. Ten minutes later she hobbled up the steps and sat down by me. I regarded her swollen knee with awe. "I'm putting ice on it," she said. "Be back in the game by the second half."

Now there's a liberal education! A little French for the mind, a little music for the soul, a few business classes to provide some tools, and then a little soccer to teach you that the swelling will go down, the pain can be endured, and you can continue to play the game.

I encourage the development of gentle people for the world of work. But if gentle people are to survive, they must be ready to put on the helmet for battle, alert for the first kick, and know that the swelling will go down. Gentleness is still the virtue for the long haul, but I want my children to have the gladiators' tools, because without them there is no long haul.

AVOIDING THE MOTOR

ON LAKE PEPIN, WHERE I SAIL, THERE ARE THREE BOATS almost like mine. They come from the same manufacturer; the only difference is that the other boats are two feet longer. One of them I have seen only once, when she passed by as I was on a dock. Another I have seen dozens of times, on both the dock and the water. *Gabrielle* is her name, and I have been puzzled by *Gabrielle* until now.

Shorter boats tend to be slower than longer boats. This is especially true if they come from the same manufacturer and have the same shape. So I have always expected that my boat, the *Laughing Buddha*, could never catch *Gabrielle*, but she always does. Our boats usually meet on the water when there is not much wind, and I have always wondered why her owners, Duke and Shirley, do not put a bigger sail on the front of *Gabrielle* when the winds are light. Frequently I will be sailing and they will have given up on the wind and be using their motor. Why not put up more sail?

The answer came to me yesterday. The wind was light, and I spotted the other boat of our design on the lake. I caught up to her quickly, as I should not have been able to do. She was flying a small sail on the front. As I came alongside, her owner dropped her sails and started her motor. I finally figured it out. For some reason, when you buy the bigger boat, they don't sell you a large front sail. And then I remembered. My boat wasn't supposed to have one either. I had ordered it specially.

I was lucky. It's more fun to sail than to motor, and

more cost-effective, and kinder to the environment, and after all, a sailboat was designed to sail.

I went out to Northland Computers the other day. The president had called me because the sales team wasn't working well. "I heard that you are a wizard," he said. I told him that sometimes it looks like I am, but I'm not really. I just know some things that most people either don't know or forget to apply. He thought he might have to fire the sales manager and maybe the whole team, although he had some hope for one of the old-timers and for a new person who had just joined the team.

I interviewed everybody and began to suggest adjustments. The first of these "wizardly" adjustments offered during a meeting with the sales manager and the president was that the president talk to the sales manager on a regular basis. The president had been in the business almost his entire life but was withholding his knowledge so that he could better judge whether or not the sales manager could make it on his own. I said to him, "People can't make it on their own, at least not in these difficult circumstances. They can't make it on their own particularly if every time they make a move, they have an expert checking a hidden scorecard for them, not telling if he approves or disapproves, waiting to suddenly fire them when it all adds up wrong."

I can't tell you how often I meet businesspeople who have little understanding of human aerodynamics. As soon as there is light air, as soon as their team experiences a little difficulty, confusion, or drop in motivation, as soon as the numbers are a little off, they reach for the starter button and drop the sails. They forget about trying to understand the people they work with and try to overpower them by punishing, shaming, or frightening them, or by setting up some silly award program, manipulating a political advantage, or even firing everybody and starting over.

People will get you places faster and cheaper—and it will be more fun—if you put as much energy into understanding them as a good sailor puts into understanding his boat. What motivates them? What training do they need? What changes would make it possible for them to improve? What sails need to be added?

About the only thing as ugly and inefficient as a sailboat squatting across the lake under the power of its motor is a group of people working under fear and coercion.

THE UNION

IN OUR HOUSE, AS I WAS GROWING UP, THE WORD *UNION* was spoken with reverence. "The union" referred to Local 340 of the United Plumbers and Pipefitters, or the gas-company union. It was the bargaining unit for most of the Minneapolis Gas Company. My father was the president.

Many unions in those days had business agents, full-time professionals, running the union. The president was an elected figurehead. Dad's union wasn't like that. He truly ran the union. At five-eight, he was not tall; he was of normal weight for a small-boned man, and not particularly strong. Yet he dominated that group of men as thoroughly as John L. Lewis dominated the mine workers or Jimmy Hoffa the Teamsters.

It's hard to go against a man who tends to be right. Charlie did his homework. I knew that because night after night our kitchen table was covered with paper: contractual clauses, insurance programs, grievances in process, company reports, pension plans. If you challenged Charlie, it was best to have your numbers handy. He had his in his head, and he would drown you with them.

He told me once, "John, the union is not about money. It's about respect." He only gave half a damn about the money. He could use it, but he had learned to live with what he had. What he cared about was that moment when he sat opposite the company negotiators and laid his demands—not requests—on the table. The company, represented by its president, Jerry Mullin, a wealthy, college-educated former state senator, listened with respect because Charlie Cowan had his facts together and, more importantly, had every dirt-digging, pipe-screwing, wrench-pulling, broom-shoving, truck-driving employee of the company behind him, ready to put down his shovel, pipe, wrench, or broom the moment he felt he was not getting a fair hearing and a fair response. They were behind Charlie, and he was behind them.

At the Minneapolis Gas Company, people did not get fired without a sound reason. The union backed them. Jobs were not laid on casually without recompense. The union asked, "What have you got him doing that for?" If you were a drunk, deserving to be dumped, the union president drove you to Willmar to get you spin-dried and the grievance committee tried to fast-talk the company out of firing you. And if you had cancer, someone from the union visited you at the hospice. I know. I waited in the car.

This strangely knurled knob of oak that was my father once said to me, "These young people. They don't get it. They think things were always good. They think management is on their side. The day the union dies, things will go back to the way they were."

You have to understand. He liked Jerry Mullin. I'd almost say he adored him. This was not personal. His point was that unchecked power is not good for anybody, and that powerlessness rots the human spirit. Every day I believe him more and more.

The only times I've done dirty-fingernail work have been during summer vacations from college. When I began working as a corporate professional years later, I felt as if I had taken a step down. There was no union for people with white shirts and ties, and little respect either.

The first time I had an appointment interrupted because my host received a summons to his boss's office, I couldn't believe it. "What's he want?" I asked.

"I don't know."

"Did he say it was an emergency?"

"No, but I better go. He's my boss, you know."

A gas-company laborer would not have put down his shovel and come running if his boss wanted to see him. I doubt if he would have put down his cigarette. He would come when there was a reasonable moment to do it. If it was that important that his boss speak to him, his boss damn well knew where he was and could come to him.

I remember the blue car with *Minnegasco* and its bright blue flame painted on the side pulling up by our work site one day. The supervisor, our boss's boss, stepped out for his weekly visit to our crew. He looked up and down the open trench at the completed pipe job on the bottom. "Think you got enough grade on that?" he asked.

"Hey, Floyd," the pipefitter hollered from the main hole where he was putting on the final connection, "If I laid it, it's got a quarter bubble on it. The only reason they made you a supervisor was that you don't know shit from shinola about fitting pipe. Don't be making noises about my work."

Floyd laughed with the rest of us. If he had wanted to use his power to get back at the pipefitter, he couldn't have, unless the pipefitter did bad work. Friendly insults were part of the game. I contrast that to the subservience I see in the professional world. The laughter at the boss's clumsy attempts at humor. The excessive respect for the boss's ideas. The back-breaking attempts to satisfy the boss's whims. The guys in the union would be flabbergasted. They always thought the white-collar world was better then theirs.

Further along now in my own career, I consult to people in positions similar to Jerry Mullin's. On the whole, I like them. They are intelligent, well-meaning people. Very few of them intend to intimidate. Several of them are even unaware of their power. Only a few are bullies.

They are not the source of the problem. They have been given unchecked power, so ugly things happen. I do not think these executives can solve the problem. No one can give another person dignity. Dignity is self-imposed. Respect is established by the person seeking respect. It is given only to those who expect it.

It does make me wish, some days, that we still had a union behind us.

COMMUNITY

———❂———

THIS SEEMS TO ME A GOOD TIME TO TALK ABOUT COMMU-
nity. I am sitting at a picnic table in Bayfield, Wisconsin,
my boat, the *Laughing Buddha*, tied to a dock fifty feet
away. My wife has just left for home. We spent a week
together sailing from marina to island to marina. I know
of no other person who could bear me so well, and whom
I could bear so well, in the confines of a very small boat
on a very large lake. As she rolls away in a carryall with
friends, her planned but sudden absence awakens the
loneliness I feel without her.

There is a cult movie, *Pow Wow Highway*, that tells the
story of two young Native American men who travel south
from Montana together to rescue a friend and sister from a
New Mexico jail. One of them is a handsome, vibrant
community organizer seeking to lift his people from economic and political oppression; the other is six feet three
inches and three hundred pounds of pulsating flesh, a
happy heart trying to flip his way through life. They are
united by the organizer's need for a car and the other's possession of one—a fifty-dollar junker bought to be the "war
pony" for his vision quest. Inevitably, their styles clash,
and in a moment of irritation, the up-and-coming leader of
his people snarls at the huge hulk behind the wheel, "With
everything bad that happens to us, with impoverishment,
sickness, and pain, how do you stay so happy?"

The response is simple: "No matter what kind of shit
comes down, I always remember that I am a Cheyenne.
No one can take that from me!"

I ask you now, in our current time and system, where do we go to find a sense of community like that?

Jim Chee, the Navajo tribal cop created by mystery writer Tony Hillerman, struggles to decide if he should accept an appointment to the FBI in Washington or remain on the reservation and be trained as a singer (something like a shaman), like his uncle before him. His white girlfriend suggests that he do both. Chee cannot find the words to explain to her that not only can a Navajo not be a singer in Washington, but that apart from the rest of his people, he cannot be a Navajo.

Does it not seem that we of this year and place are missing something? That we who are dislocated from a larger clan, living as nomadic individuals, are not quite human? That we are parts without a whole?

I have not always felt this loneliness. I am both a Swede and an Irishman, and as a child I was equally proud of being one or the other. As a church person I was confident in the rectitude of my tribe against all others. That pride and sense of belonging was set aside as I launched a more sophisticated life.

I have felt this sense of community emerging in a couple of business units to which I have belonged—but barely, and only for a moment. Then the pressures of business life intervened, the organization changed and we all went in different directions. From these experiences I collected friends, but not a community.

I have now moved from the picnic table to the cabin of the *Buddha*. This is a very dirty boat. It must be cleaned. I have no more time to respond to this yearning of my heart, nor do I think I can, here by myself, in this year and this lifetime. There is a boat to be cleaned. In that, I think, lies the problem. There are too many boats to be cleaned for us to waste our time being together, forming a greater whole.

At a Tae Kwon Do tournament I was killing time

awaiting my son's entrance into the ring by discussing this problem of community with the parents of another contestant. As we parted, one of them said, "Of course, you know that community must be earned."

I did not know that. I have been too busy cleaning boats, seeking clients, and writing books to have time to give to others. I've had too much to do to create or even commit to a group of people. I haven't earned my community.

THE EDUCATION OF A RADICAL

—————— ✕ ——————

IN THE MOVIE *GREEN CARD* THE HEROINE ACCUSES THE hero of being "right-wing." "No, it is you that have wings," he responds. "All your ideas come from one place."

My father was an Irish Catholic. My mother was a Swedish Baptist who converted to Catholicism to make my father and his family happy. My father and his family thought the Swedes stupid. My mother and her family thought the Irish mean or worse.

When I was in third grade, my grandmother Amanda explained to me that Catholics sacrificed living babies to God. When I respectfully told her that I had never seen that happen, she said that Catholics only did it in missionary countries, so the people back here wouldn't know about it. She had seen a slide show about it at her church. She had no doubt that what had been presented to her was the truth.

This did not seem very likely to me, so I checked it with my mother, who I thought would be willing to both honor grandmother's opinion and yet have the facts on what our church was doing. Of course, she told me that Grandmother was wrong on this. I had not believed Grandmother enough to feel relief. I had had enough experience with sisters, priests, and Catholic relatives to realize that even though I had reason to fear the nuns' ruler, none of them seemed like candidates for the high-priest role in a baby-sacrificing ceremony. I doubted that they would have the heart for it.

I do not know what Grandmother Amanda saw or heard that led her to think of Catholics as baby killers. She could speak three languages, but sometimes her English was not perfectly effective. Perhaps that was the root of the problem. I met her minister one day and found him not perfectly effective either, so perhaps that was it.

I do know that I was told not only by my father and his family but by the whole Roman Catholic church from the pope to Sister Mary Catherine, my third grade teacher, that all Protestants were going to hell. I assumed that included Amanda, my grandfather Emil, my uncle Ernie, and my aunt Anna—the whole incorrigible lot of them.

It did not seem likely to me that the woman who fed me cookies was going to hell. Or that my grandfather who drove me the block and a half to school when I lived at his house was destined for eternal perdition. Or that Ernie and Anna, who welcomed me at their house whenever I chose, who invited me to eat their food, play with their dog, dig in their night-crawler pit, and steal their sons' old Big-Little Books, had everlasting fire waiting on their horizon. How could people who spoiled me rotten be doomed to eternal damnation?

This battle of verities persisted over the years. At Emil and Amanda's house it was taken for granted that I was a Swede among Swedes. (When Grandmother was dying, I had to remind her to speak English to me; she was repeatedly startled to realize that I didn't speak Swedish.) On the other side of town I was an Irish Catholic. This distinguished me from such foreign tribes as the French Catholics, German Catholics, and Italian Catholics. Further than that the Resurrection School did not go.

And both sides of the family were quite willing to explain to me in depth, whether I asked or not, how the universe worked. They were both certain. Contrary to what you might expect, I was not confused by this. I too developed my certitudes.

First, I was certain that nobody knew anything for sure, no matter how aggressively they stated their certainty or with what marvelously rational arguments they buttressed their opinions. Because no matter how convincing someone was on one day, I knew that the next day I would face an equally convincing person on the other side of the debate with different arguments, different facts, and similar aggressiveness and certainty.

Second, I was certain that most people do not want to hear anything different than what they currently believe. The Irish never argued with the Swedes, and the Swedes never talked to the Irish. They just knew the other side was intractable. My mother would laugh and say, "Stubborn Irishman"; my father would grumble, "Hard-headed Swede." Sometimes I would try to help by telling one side or the other, in as peaceful a tone and with as rational a rhetoric as possible, what the other side felt. I eventually learned not to do that anymore.

Third, I was certain that all this opinion made not much difference at all in practice. I played with toy trucks on the floor of the Irish mansion belonging to Lena and Jim with the same comfort in which I read comics on Amanda and Emil's front porch. Amanda fed me. My other grandmother, Liza Feeney Cowan, told me long and rambling stories of living in the North Woods. They were all kind and wonderful people.

Fourth, I was certain that I was never going to die for a bunch of words. The Swedes would die for the Bible, the Catholics for the Trinity. I preferred living.

My childhood experience has shaped me and left me with some rules for living and working.

Every time I hear of the latest panacea, from the "Total Quality" movement of today back to "Management by Objectives," the program of choice when I entered business, I try to avoid giggling in the zealot's face. Whatever the program, it will not have the effect its evangelists claim for it.

On the other hand, I never throw one of these ideas away. MBO is a dirty word in many organizations now, but I still advocate its use. It is no more or less effective than it ever was. In my opinion it is still valuable with some amendments learned through the history of its application. Ten years from now I expect I will still announce Deming's gospel of continuous improvement— not with the fervor of today's disciples, but I expect by then they will be gone. I am still in favor of productivity measures—I once even constructed a course on them— although productivity measurers are not around today in a fraction of the force they were ten years ago.

I never believe people who tell me someone else is unreasonable. I expect that when I get to know the devil in the next division, the autocrat of operations, and the old witch in accounting, I am going to find people living perfectly reasonably within their own worlds, with their own facts, reasons, and arguments.

Sometimes, I admit, I am a bit uncomfortable, embarrassed at being quiet when others are adamant. It does seem a little weak. Sometimes I wish that my voice could harden with the ring of conviction I hear in others. But it can't. I have discarded half of my own opinions over the last decade. Which of those I hold now will go into the trash in the decade to come?

I am an advocate for the tentative approach. Let's hear the other opinion. Let's talk to our adversaries. Let's not put all our eggs in one basket. Let's be slower to judge. I have never met anyone who was either all wrong or all right.

THE WINDS OF CHANGE

———— ✥ ————

THE FOURTH OF JULY CAME ON A SATURDAY, SO JULY 3 WAS the closest we had to a declared national holiday. It was not a great day down on the docks of Lake Pepin. The wind was thirty knots and more, coming down the length of the lake from the west. On the Beaufort scale it is called Force 5, which won't knock down a building but will make a mess of a lake.

Several of us sailboaters gathered off and on out at the seawall to look and decide again if we were right to stay in the harbor or if there might be some fun out there after all. Ross said it best: "It's the type of day you can survive if you are caught in it, but it makes no sense to get out there on purpose." A couple of the bigger sailboats did go out. The rest of us watched them and felt quite confirmed in our decision to stay ashore. It looked like war.

The winds of change are blowing through organizations. The companies to which I consult have programs for change. They are installing new ways of conducting the business, cutting the fat and at times some of the bone. Government entities have less money with which to get the same services done and face a public that is not only unsympathetic but more demanding. I know no organization that is not facing the winds of change. As workers, we either bear these winds or we sit in the harbor. Paychecks are not distributed for sitting in the harbor.

As a sailor, I have some hints for surviving and even

enjoying high winds. While the huge powerboats go out in any weather, sailboats go out in weather that most normal-sized powerboats avoid. We are built for that kind of stuff. We have high sides, weighted keels, and covered decks. So here is a small-boat sailor—mine is only twenty-three feet long—giving some advice on living out your time in the winds of change.

I was frustrated that July 3. For the Fourth I had to return to the city and I did want to sail before I left. By the evening the wind had dropped slightly, maybe just enough, I thought, to make the critical difference. At eight I saw two of my friends walking down A Dock toward their boat, four slips down from mine. I told them I had a question to which I hoped they would answer no. Would they like to go sailing? They said that they had been sitting in a restaurant deciding whether to order pie or come down and see if I was ready to go. I was. We went.

That is my first piece of advice: *Have friends who are sailors.* When the winds of change are blowing, there are a lot of people seeking your friendship who are not sailors. They want to complain about how tough it is out there, and they are perfectly correct. It is tough out there. But they want to sit in the harbor and curse the wind. Friends who are sailors may curse the wind from time to time, but they are interested, excited at the prospect of taking advantage of it. They look for the hole in the gale, the crack in the storm, and they encourage you to slip out of the harbor, set the sails, and blast across the lake. They not only encourage you, they sail with you, as Mark and Sandy did with me.

Once you're on the boat, the first step is to *shorten the sails.* Full sails are for light winds. Before we left the dock, we took off the large genoa, the front sail, and replaced it with a much smaller working jib. We shortened the mainsail. Mainsails can be rigged so that they don't go all the way up the mast. We tied her down to two-thirds of her normal size.

In a changing organization, get your ambitions down to size. Put a reef in your projects. Go for the short-term completion date. Don't think five years ahead; nothing will be the same then. That job you've got your eye on for five years from now won't be there. If you have a technology that will take five years to install, install it in short cycles, making each cycle a success in itself. Too much sail in a big wind puts the boat on its side. Chopping away at projects that can be completed allows you to advance, and when the wind shifts, to leave behind you accomplishments, not half-done and half-baked dreams.

Now you must go sailing. It will calm your nerves. The waves look insurmountable from the dock. Even as we three turn out of the harbor under power and feel the full effects of the wind, it remains scary. But the moment the sails are set, the boat establishes her angle of heel. She begins to move forward in her own manner. I remember that this is her natural element. This is what she was built for. My heart calms. My pipe is lit. I grab a cup of coffee and lean against her side as she rises and falls in the swells and the wind that terrified me from the dock now drives us forward. "Tiller feels light," Mark says.

"Want more power from the main?" I reply. Sandy gives me a nod, and I adjust the traveler in. The main takes a fuller bite of the wind, and the *Buddha* surges ahead. *The wind feels lighter when you are sailing.* And scarier when you are hiding.

I had a colleague in a changing organization who was distracted by the wind whistling in the rigging. "I think Frank does not want this to happen." "I hear they are thinking of closing this account anyway." "Have you heard that maybe another division might try to do this and they might be better at it?" When things are changing, this type of static can always be heard. Maybe Frank does not want this to happen. Maybe they will close the account. Maybe the other division will try to do it. And maybe they won't. Having rabbit ears is fatal when the winds of change are howling.

I learned early that when I was changing a sail in a storm, there were important things occurring around me that might effect my well-being. Yes, that thumping noise may very well be the portable toilet tipping over, but do not pay attention to it now. Focus on putting this sail on this wire, and when you're done, and only when you're done, see if your cabin smells like a sewer. Usually it turns out that it was just a noise. Usually all the distracting noises in an organization in flux turn out to be just noises. *Focus on what you are trying to do.* Do it. Rack it up as accomplished. Then move on to the next thing.

Know where safety is and how to get to it. We covered a good chunk of lake that evening, but the entire time I knew what I had to do to return to the harbor or ride out the blow if conditions worsened. If we dropped the jib, we would survive double the wind we faced. If we turned and ran, Pepin's blinking navigation light would welcome us home. If forced, we would sail through the entrance, and with three of us working the problem we would be under power in our home harbor within a minute or two.

Stay in touch with the boss. Make sure she will provide a safety net in trouble. Know how you will salvage most of the work if changing winds doom the project. Seek allies who will stand up for you as you stand up for them. Don't try to go too far on your own. These are not the times to alienate unnecessarily the powers that be. Look at what you might do if you did not work for your organization. People, good people, get cut just because somebody had to go. Be prepared for it, and it won't sink you.

Calculated risks work well in heavy seas. Careless risks get you killed. *Place your bets, but hedge them.*

We had a lovely sail. With everything up and rigged for the wind, we drove down the lake straight into the sunset, lifting and sliding through the waves. If somebody had offered me a forty-two-foot cabin cruiser on the spot in exchange for my little boat, I would not have accepted the offer. I don't want to be insulated from this kind of beauty. If somebody had told me she had the power to wave her hand and drop the wind from twenty-five knots to ten and lower the waves from three feet to ripples, I would have asked her to be still and not interfere. I was having too much fun doing it this way.

About a half hour after dark we brought the *Laughing Buddha* back to the marina, knocked down the sails, put her under power, rode the swells through the entrance, and made the turn for the run up the channel, between the docks, toward my slip. I took the tiller from Mark, for two reasons. On the open water, no matter who is at the tiller, the owner captains the boat. But in the harbor there are objects to be collided with, and other sailors prefer that the captain be directly responsible for his own collisions. That's why Mark gave me the tiller. The reason I took it was that we were about to promenade through the entire Pepin fleet and I wanted it perfectly clear whose boat weathered that storm and which sailor had had the skill to do it. So I took the tiller in one hand and stood on the seat where I could see ahead but, even more importantly, be seen by the tied-down boats we were passing. I suspect that many were saying, "Here comes that silly old man again, showing off!" They're right. It sure is silly, but, God, does it feel *good!*

ENTERING AUTUMN

IT IS THE LABOR DAY WEEKEND, AND A FEW OF US ARE SITting around inside the marina building at Pepin, drinking coffee from Styrofoam cups. Joe says that he feels winter is coming early. There isn't any argument. People speak of the various signs they are observing, from the chill in the air to the hint of color turning in the trees and the hue of the sumac. I don't argue either, although I am not too certain that any of those signs have anything to do with the coming of winter. Maybe they do. I defer to superior knowledge.

Instead I start thinking about my own personal winter, and the autumn that is preceding it.

I am now fifty-seven years old.

My biggest fear and concern is when my winter will come. The Irish males in my family die with cancer somewhere around their seventieth birthday. This has been true of my grandfather, my uncle, and my father, which makes up the whole Irish lot of them. On the other hand, the Swedes last forever. My Swedish grandfather died at ninety-seven, and as near as I can figure out, he only decided to die because he was getting bored.

If I have only fifteen years left, I better get cracking with whatever I want to do. Death is dramatically close. On the other hand, if I have forty years left, what am I doing even considering this topic? This isn't autumn, this is the middle of summer.

Not one to take chances, I am going to assume that autumn is here. What do I do with it? What is autumn's

task? It is not about perfecting my body. The body is slipping. So be it. Last spring I hauled my new outboard
motor out of my trunk and painfully carried it a few feet
toward the docks. Joe called one of his sons to carry it the
rest of the way for "Mr. Cowan." Twenty years ago he
wouldn't have considered such a move. Ten years ago he
might have offered help, but I wouldn't have considered
accepting. Two years ago I would have let him do it but
felt bad about my slipping prowess. This year I was thankful, and open in my admiration for the young man who
picked it up, threw it on his shoulder, and hiked the two
blocks to my boat without even raising a sweat. My body
is slipping. So be it. The task of autumn is not perfecting
the body.

I do not think the task of autumn is even the perfec-
tion of the personality. I feel content with being myself. I
have chipped away for a long time at the block provided
by my parents, and there isn't much more chipping to be
done. The sculpture is not perfect, but you are not going
to hear a lot of hammering from this corner. My hammer
is weary, my chisel blunted, and the old block is getting
tired of the pounding.

I have been given two hints as to autumn's task. First, I
am beginning to enjoy myself as a unique product. I take
delight in being the particular blend of experiences that I
am. When I was twenty, there were many others who
came from essentially the same mold. Now, with all the
twists and turns life takes, I am sure that there is no one
who resembles me.

Second, I am tired of ageist jokes. I go to others' thirti-
eth, fortieth, and fiftieth birthday parties wary of the
black crepe, black balloons, and cynical cards. It seems so
childish to mock the process of growth, so blind to not
see behind the wrinkles the surging of a spirit, so wasteful
to spend time mourning the decay of the body rather
than acknowledging the growth of the person.

Once, when I was in my thirties, I was trapped in a group of people who were passing around the pictures from someone's family reunion. I found myself quickly passing on the pictures of the attractive young and slowing to study the wrinkles of the old for clues to the life that had created their faces, to search for the outline of the indelible soul emerging because of the erosion of the body.

And here, finally, is the task of autumn: to clearly present to the world the unique spirit that has been nurtured within. Now is the time to set aside the cosmetic supports of eternal youth, the tarp of merely facile charm, and uncover the sculpture of the essential self, however life has thumped it into shape.

WHAT ARE FRIENDS FOR?

———— ✦✕✦ ————

FIVE YEARS AGO, AS I WAS STANDING ON THE LAKE SIDE OF the marina building, Joe asked me what I thought of the idea of turning the ice cream and sundries area into a restaurant. I had no idea how that could be done, since for me floor plans are fixed forever. I cannot visualize the moving of walls or even the moving of furniture. But the business concept appealed to me.

Soon after that Joe remodeled the marina building and turned most of it into a neat little restaurant. Some powerboaters came, along with many sailors from the marina and some people from the town. By me, it has been just fine. After two years Joe leased the place to Dorothy. It is now called Dorothy's Ship's Wheel. At the same time that Joe started the Ship's Wheel on one end of the marina, at the other end an old building was remodeled and another restaurant, the Pickle Factory, was installed. I don't know if it was so named because the old building was a pickle factory or because it's a good place to go if you wish to get pickled. I know little about it because I have always refused to go there.

My attitude toward the Pickle Factory is not completely reasonable. I am a little annoyed that its patrons park on marina property. There is ample parking, and they do not get in my way, but it offends my sense of justice that the marina blacktop, which cost a fair amount of money, is supporting Pickle Factory cars. I also find irritating the fact that after the marina closes in the evening and marina personnel are no longer on hand to collect the couple of bucks owed for tying up, several powerboats pull in, one usually on the end of my dock, and laugh their way off to the Pickle Factory. Somewhere around eleven they wake me up as they thunder down the dock, kick over motors that belch like 727s, and roar back to their home ports. I resent being wakened. I resent their cheating the marina out of a couple of bucks. And I blame it all on the Pickle Factory.

However, the underlying reason for my never turning right but always turning left when I leave the dock is that Joe, Sue, Neil, and Dorothy are my friends. When I spend my money, I spend my money in ways that support my friends. I do not spend my money on their competitors. This may be an old-fashioned peculiarity on my part, or a remnant from my clerical days. Or perhaps it's one of the psychological anomalies of being raised in what is now called a dysfunctional family. I remain, however, fairly stubborn about it, although I have never seen it described in the business literature as a virtue.

I know I can carry my loyalty too far. On the other hand, many do not carry loyalty far enough. They operate as if business were a pure chess game. If you are up and valuable to them, you are their friend. If you are down, too bad. They may not step on you, but they will certainly ignore you.

Some of my friends started a select group for consultants. There were about six of us. Saddled with my own principles, I asked that we commit to attend every meeting. "No, no," was the response. "It's too important to take advantage of business opportunities. We will understand if anyone cancels coming to a meeting because of business." I didn't like this much, but I thought I could live with it, since these were my friends and getting together with them was helpful under any circumstances. I thought that until one April day when I arrived at a meeting prepared to confide in them that my business had been doing terribly, that I was deeply shaken, did not know if I could make it out of the jam, and needed their help.

Instead of five other people at the meeting, there were only two. The other three were too occupied making money to have time to hear that I was not. These people remain my friends, but I quit the group. I never want to experience those feelings again. I dug my own way out of the April business hole. I see them one at a time, when they can commit to seeing me.

On the other hand, I am helping a YPO (Young President's Organization) group that has been together for several years. Lateness costs a few dollars; missing a meeting costs about twenty. The money is simply a reminder that the obligation to one another is to be taken seriously. These young presidents find consistent value in this organization because they act as friends to one another even when there is no obvious short-term advantage in doing so.

Shortly before I began to work with them, one of their number was in trouble in his own company. He called his fellow YPO members one evening and had half of them show up for a special meeting to help him the next morning. These men are presidents of good-sized corporations. Their calendars are not easily cleared. Yet they were there.

I had a terrible thing happen the other day. I heard *Kristina* call for a temporary berth in the Pepin harbor. I got on my own radio and asked Ron and Bev where they were going, told them I would love to join them. They were going to the Pickle Factory. I did join them, but I only drank water. This was not purely out of smallness—I was thirsty and not ready to eat. I hate to tell you this. It is a pleasant place. However, I had heard that the food was poor, so I remained content in my decision to never go there. Until last week, when my adventurous wife suggested that since I had eaten breakfast at Dorothy's, maybe I could bear having lunch at the Pickle Factory.

Mostly to prove to her that I can get out of a rut if I have to (something she doubts), I went, and ordered a hamburger with lettuce, mayonnaise, and tomato. It was good.

I may go there again. But I will not go there frequently. My loyalties swing me to the left as I leave the dock. If I turn right, I will do it reluctantly and seldom. I put my energies and my money with my friends, not their competitors.

The other day, Joe and Sue's son, Matt, fixed the wiring to my radio, instantly and for free. "No big deal," he said, waving off my thanks, "What are friends for?"

THANKSGIVING

———————— ⊰✷⊱ ————————

THANKSGIVING DAY IS COMING.

About ten years ago, in anticipation of this day, some people began wishing me a Happy Turkey Day. This phrase entered my life in such a genuine and jovial tone that for the first couple of dozen times I didn't give it much thought. I assumed I was being wished a Happy Thanksgiving. Realization came first with a jolt, then with revulsion.

I don't like turkey. I eat it because as a chronically fat man I eat whatever isn't fattening, but I don't like it. When I woke up to the fact that these people were wishing me happiness in eating one of those stringy, corn-gulping, filthy-feathered, ill-tasting birds, every beneficent outpouring of their good will brought from me a gurgle of intestinal protest. I would not have thought about this further if they had wished me Happy Filet Mignon Day, or Happy Boiled and Buttered Shrimp Day, or, dream of my dreams, Happy Unlimited Supply of Whiskey and Water Accompanied by Quantities of Pickled Herring on Ritz Crackers Until Your Wife Puts You to Bed in a Drunken Stupor Day. But they offered me none of these most happy days. They offered me a Happy Turkey Day. So I did think about it further. What have they got against Thanksgiving?

Maybe they don't believe in God, so they don't have anyone to thank. Fair enough; God is hardly an open-and-shut case. But that couldn't be it. The Pilgrims who started all this were not thanking just God, they were thanking the Indians who had rescued them from starvation by teaching them how to supply themselves with the elements of this feast. (I do hope the Native Americans present for that first feast enjoyed themselves hugely, since our relationship with them began deteriorating with the last slice of pumpkin pie.)

So, even if they do not believe in God, don't they have someone to thank, and something to thank them for? Well, now, as I thought about it, maybe they don't think they do. If I did not believe in God, would I have someone to thank and something to thank them for? I have had to struggle a fair amount with life, and I don't have many things that other people have. I could make a case for sliding by Turkey Day without gratitude. But I won't. I am very thankful to clients who will have me, friends who endure my ongoing life struggle, advice, and counsel from all corners, a wife who always stands by me, and two sons who can pick up the air conditioner I no longer can move. I am very thankful the house is warm, does not leak, and that every person in it has a TV set. I'm grateful for three cars that tend to run and the first semester paid at Augsburg College.

And I am certain that I did not create this situation myself. For some years now I have shocked those who compliment me on my various talents by accepting their compliments without a blink. I am very good at some things. I can accept that because I know full well that I have had very little to do with my talents.

Comments about my weaknesses I do not accept with the same equanimity, but I should. I have had as little to do with the fact of their existence as I have had to do with creating my own talents.

I don't know what it means to be a self-made man. If nothing else, every person who likes himself or herself must be thankful that one particular genetic pool experi-

enced a surge of blood at the sight of another particular
genetic pool's bedroom-bound bottom.

I compare myself to those I know who are most well-
heeled and famous, and I experience envy and greed. I
compare myself to most of the world, and I experience
gratitude. I have noticed that there are people starving
out there. If I were born poor and living in a different
neighborhood, my family would be carrying guns, and I
would have bought them for them, or stolen them, whatever necessity dictated.

So if you have the means to circulate in my circles and
are a member of this surreptitious campaign to stamp out
Thanksgiving by renaming it Turkey Day, please avoid
me with your well wishes. There is something about a
person who can afford an air-conditioned car being
unwilling to set aside a day to express gratitude that
spoils the taste of my pickled herring.

Somewhere along the line—maybe when my folks sent
me to college, when Honeywell hired an indigent ex-
clergyman, or when I bought my sailboat—I incurred an
obligation to thank someone for all this, and to beg him
or her to please not take it back.

BUSINESS AS CREATIVE
COMMUNITY

———— ✦✦ ————

WE RESIST THINKING OF OUR BUSINESSES AS COMMUNITIES.
Perhaps this is because we have other communities in
which we feel so much safer and we do not want to use
the same word to designate the demanding world of business and the permissive worlds of home, extended family,
club, association, and church. Not that these other
worlds, which we dignify with the word *community*, are
necessarily peaceful. I have seen more division in the
church than I have seen in business, and certainly more
open display of anger in my home than I've seen in any
business department. But in these communities we are
safe from being thrown out for any but the most grievous
of faults, whereas in business, excommunication is a readily available solution to minor flaws. During a downturn,
the hatchet may be used simply because a person is not
indispensable. It does rather keep one on edge.

I would find it hard to imagine a business that was also
a community if I had not dealt with one. But I have.
They built my kitchen. As a business, they are known as
North Star Incorporated. As a church, they are known as
Christ's Household of Faith. I am not of their religious
persuasion and have no desire to undertake the disci-
plines of their community. However, as one of their business clients, I was most impressed.

The salesman and kitchen designer worked well as a
team. They listened to my wife, the boss of our family on
such matters, with attention. They made room for one

another in the conversation. They referred to their capabilities with confidence. They were clear about what they could not do. After we approved the design, the carpenter and his assistant arrived completely briefed on what we wanted. In-process design changes were communicated to the carpenter, and he returned with designs that had been changed overnight. We were assured the taper would get it right without supervision because the carpenter planned to sit with him over supper and ensure that he had the correct message. The next day he did it right. As did the plumber, the stove installer, and the glass worker. My wife and I were totally satisfied.

On the other hand, we have been trying to build a professional hockey team in Minnesota. Normally, we don't do too well. Particularly during the regular season. All year long the coaches talk about the need for teamwork, yet the team doesn't work like a team. One of my clients had the answer. He had played hockey with the team's general manager. "He is one swell fellow. A great guy. But he doesn't understand how teams are formed. He was always interested in his own statistics. He preaches teamwork, but rewards the players for the goals they score. Now, who is going to backcheck when all the rewards are given for what happens on the offensive end of the ice?"

If you don't understand hockey, think of what happens to the New York Yankees year after year. They have one of the biggest markets in baseball. They can buy all the talent they need. But they never create a working community.

What would happen if your business tried to be a community? I don't think it ever could succeed completely, but what if you tried to get as close to the ideal as you could? I think some very good things would happen.

Your customer would experience seamless service. The trouble always comes in the handoffs. The shipping clerk doesn't feel like mailing the part to the serviceperson at the end of the day and leaves him to explain as best he can the delay to the customer. The serviceperson, in irritation at not getting support, vilifies the company to the customer, making the next sale more difficult. The salesperson does not bother to fill out the parts list accurately because he wants to move on to the next sale. People in community don't do things like that to one another.

You would stop misusing your human resources. You may think that you don't misuse your human resources. I think you probably do. For instance, I have a reputation as a writer. I am pretty good. I worked in corporations for eleven years and no one except myself knew I could write. I was a resource wasted. On the other hand, I spent much time proofreading and somehow managed to survive without anyone observing that I do not notice errors. One of the best salesmen I know spent twenty years working as an accountant. One of the best businessmen worked nearly as long as a customer engineer. People are normally hired into jobs that do not allow them to apply their full talents because it is impossible to write a job description that takes into account the full range of one person's talents without closing the job to everyone else in the universe. Be that as it may, would it not be wonderful if once people were hired, they used the full range of their talents in service of the corporation?

You would eliminate the failures caused by weaknesses of individuals. How did I survive as a proofreader without spotting errors? I always had friends who rushed into the gap to save me from my inability, just as I was always willing to offer my noncreative friends fourteen creative ways out of their problems. In community, people take care of one another and in the process create a better product.

Energy would be aimed at accomplishing tasks instead of protecting and promoting image. In a community, people are known to one another. Image creation is hopeless, so it is soon abandoned. There is a level of safety in which a member will be accepted, warts and all. The task itself, not how it looks to others, becomes what is important.

People would be empowered. Much powerlessness arises from the mistaken notion that the boss knows best. Only some of the time is that so. Somebody else knows best most of the time. In a community, people develop a clear notion of one another's capabilities, irrespective of titles. Soon they understand what things the boss knows best and what they know best. A side effect of this phenomenon is that people become more docile. When the boss really does know best, employees don't argue, they just cooperate.

As my father used to say, "'Tain't easy, McGee!" But I think building a sense of community is worth it. Much of the waste in business comes from the arm's-length relationships. That is where the hypocrisy is created. That is where the ball is dropped. That is where mistakes happen. In the arm-and-arm relationships of community the ball is passed, the bullshit confronted, the errors corrected. Besides that, it is nice to get up in the morning and go to a place where most of the people like you, support you, help you, a place where the smiles are genuine.

EVIL

I WAS STARTLED ONE DAY ABOUT A YEAR AGO WHEN A friend of mine said that I did not believe in evil. I had never given it a moment's thought. I responded with things like "Sorta," "Maybe," and "I'm not sure." I had been trained to believe in evil. How could I not? And yet, maybe I didn't. I have mulled over this possibility and chewed on its consequences for at least a year. I now feel that my friend was right: I do not believe in evil.

I do believe that there are damaging things I do not want to have happen to me, violent people I want to avoid, stupid ideas I do not want holding sway. But to me the word *evil* connotes something or someone purposely malevolent. Whenever I have examined closely and fearlessly something or somebody that I thought to be evil, I have found reason to see that the "evil" persons involved were benevolent in their intentions, once I understood their vision of the world.

When I was young, wolves were thought of as evil. They malevolently killed deer, and deer were good, cute, and graceful. Wolves skulked and sneaked, both evil acts. But now the wolf has been redeemed. Books and movies have shown what lovable animals they are, merely pursuing their supper by weeding out aged and ill deer. Mostly, wolves eat mice, and everybody knows mice are evil. Mice skulk and sneak.

When asked how it felt to play an evil man, Charlton Heston once stated, "I never play an evil man, for no man sees himself as evil. If I empathize with the character, I do things the character sees as good. Others see these actions as evil."

I do not believe in evil people because I have never met one. Anytime I have thought someone evil, or even bad, and have been given the barest glimpse of how that person sees the world, or what the world has done to that person, I experience compassion. In eight years of hearing confessions, some of them in a lockup psychiatric ward, I did not run into a malevolent person. I did encounter many pathetic people, sadly caught in their own dilemmas, and some dangerous ones—one of whom spat in my face when I declined his invitation to release him from his restraints. I did not think him evil. Restrain me, and I'll get nasty too. Nor did I release him. I did think him dangerous.

I do not think my point of view is Christian. It is perhaps Buddhist, and certainly Taoist, so I am not without some support. It is also Aristotelian and Thomistic. That school of psychology taught that the will seeks whatever the intellect presents to it as the good. The will is benevolent, not malevolent. It is the intellect's mistaken world view that is the cause of the negative act.

Part of the genius of Christianity is its ability to simplify life into good and evil, thereby giving the good permission to destroy the evil. (We Christians are not the only ones to do this, we're just the most successful.) We have accumulated wealth and conquered territory by our capacity to see the features of the devil in the faces of other tribes, hear his threatening voice from their throats, and see his madness blazing in their eyes.

The Israelites destroyed their neighbors. The Crusaders destroyed the heathen. White men destroyed red men. Irish Catholics destroy Irish Protestants. Irish Protestants destroy Irish Catholics. Business attacks government. Government attacks business. Department attacks department. Colleague attacks colleague. If evil did not exist, permission for this destruction and attack would not be given. But if it does exist, and if we think we have found it, we have permission to excise it. And if someone thinks us evil, he or she has permission to terminate us. I once knew a holy nun who had seen the devil incarnate in a human being. Unfortunately, I was that human being. Fortunately, she was powerless.

No, thanks. I don't believe in evil. Don't convince me. I don't want to believe. The belief in evil is a dangerous thing. It promotes attack and counterattack. If we hope to create anything different, we must start with some other assumption.

If we do not believe in evil, then we must look at any situation long enough to discover its true cause. With that discovery comes the possibility of a cure. Sure, she might be undercutting you because she is evil. But if you look long enough to know that she is afraid you are after her job, you can do something to fix the situation. Sure, everybody at the corporate level is evil, but what if they simply do not understand your division? You can change that for the better. Sure, all those who block your will are evil. But what if the real problem is that sometimes you are wrong, that your will deserves to be blocked? Now *there* is an evil that could easily be fixed.

THE HEAT OF THE GAME

THE FIRST THING YOU MUST UNDERSTAND IS THAT ROMAN Catholic seminarians of the late fifties were not quite the sweet bunch of guys you might think them. We came mostly from the blue-collar class and were rather macho jocks with finely honed competitive instincts. One of our hidden reasons for accepting a call to the church was our desire to get ahead in the world we understood most. Being a priest ranked ahead of any other career. We were aiming for the top of the ladder as seen by ourselves, our families, and our friends. So when we engaged in recreational activities, we did so with gusto and ferocity. We were a competitive bunch.

For a short while, some of my classmates and I took pleasure in crossing Summit Avenue to the St. Thomas pool to play an informal game of water polo, without rules except for where the ball must go to count for a goal. Although played in water, these games grew hotter by the week. One day I was tracking down a ball in nine feet of water when my friend John Webb came over my back. John and I had been matched against each other in almost every sport for ten years, but despite that, or maybe because of it, he did not hesitate to drive me underwater and swim over my head, with a few resounding thumps to the noggin from his thrashing feet, in order to take possession of the ball.

When I came to the surface, he had just grabbed the ball. He didn't yet have a firm grip on it and was not yet ready to relay it to one of his teammates. His back was to me, so I caught him by the shoulders, drove him under the water, and perched comfortably on his squirming body. "Now," I thought, "we will stay like this until the ball comes to the surface." Since I had caught him by surprise and he was short of oxygen, that took only about fifteen seconds. "Now," I thought, "I will perch here until he stops squirming." Another fifteen seconds passed before I realized that I was trying to kill him.

I let him up. The game went on, and I am not sure that Webb realized how close he came to being dead or how close I came to having a sudden career change from priest to lifer in the penitentiary. In the parking lot afterward I suggested that we find another use for our Saturday afternoons. The guy who had temporarily lost the use of his right arm because of this game seconded the motion. The guy who could no longer see out of his left eye thought I had something there. And the two lifelong friends who had had their fight broken up by the lifeguard added weight to the argument simply by ignoring the discussion and continuing to glare at each other. So we quit.

Which is something business does not let us do. Business sneaks up on me. The scars and abrasions are not quite so obvious—particularly since the wounded are expected to conceal their pain.

In business most of us start with the best of intentions, planning only to make a living and live a life. But the game is seductive. Some see power and wealth at the goal line and become increasingly short-tempered and vicious the closer the score seems to come, although it never comes, remaining always a few inches from their clutching fingers. I have never felt that, but I have seen it. What I have felt is my hatred for losing. I need not win, but losing drives me wild. So although I never hoped for greater power and wealth, I nonetheless become short-tempered and vicious in making sure that whatever I have been assigned to do comes out precisely as I have told my superiors it would.

As a program manager for a major corporation I once turned down the bill from a small consulting company for two thousand dollars. They had submitted it six months late. I had told them twice at the end of the year to get the bills in because I was closing the project, was assured twice that all was settled, and then in June this bill had arrived. I told them I was not paying it, that I had no account to pay it from, the project was closed, it was on budget, and I was done talking about it. Cowan is on standard, on budget, and on time, and they can damn well be the same.

In the broader picture, which I can see well now but could not in the heat of the game, the money meant next to nothing to my corporation and meant quite a bit to a tiny vendor. I could have found it in some other account without trying very hard. Three months later the vendor-relations department paid them from their account after months of argument and documentation. But it was the heat of the game that seduced me. (Justice is being served. Now that I am a small-time vendor, I'm the one who is running into uptight corporate program managers knocking me down for five hundred bucks here and a thousand there.)

You can quit playing water polo. In business it is harder to play the game and govern the competitive instincts. I cannot quit and continue to raise a family. At least once a day something comes along in which someone can win and someone can lose. Instead of taking the reasonable approach to finding a common solution, I find my competitive needs turning on my adrenaline and my mind racing for a tactic that will drown the other guy. As long as I play this or any other game, the temptations will be there.

A practice we had in the seminary was to every night

mentally review the day to see how we had screwed up. It was a little morbid, perhaps, but I still do it and find it effective. Another thing I am finding helpful is that finally I am beginning to recognize the competitive urge before it hits me. Having a name for it helps. For a long time I thought I was just doing business. But now I think of it as that homicidal urge and recognize that there are alternative ways to ensure a better conclusion.

Perhaps the thing that helps most is having enough personal history to know that in the long run these victories have not done me much good. In one corporation, when my boss had repeated to a colleague my ten devastating reasons for canceling that colleague's project, that colleague won his point by saying: "Everybody knows Cowan is against anything he did not create and is deadly when he shoots it down." I must say that although he exaggerated some, I had won enough battles to deserve that counterpunch. He scored, and I had the good sense to back off.

So I am getting better at this. I cannot quit this game of business. I don't want to quit. But year by year I feel less of an urge to drown my competition.

CRIPPLED HAWK

———— ✕ ————

MY NAME IS CRIPPLED HAWK. IT IS NOT THE NAME YOU will see on the front of this book or in any other reference to me. It is not my public name but my spiritual name.

I was born in 1935. My parents were an Irish-Catholic man, a banker's son destined to spend most of his life in jobs too menial for his intelligence, and a Swedish Baptist woman, struggling to have the fine things she always wanted when she was scrubbing the floor as one of nine kids on a dirt-poor farm in central Minnesota. I was a quick-witted boy inhabiting a fat and clumsy body and living in an emotionally crippling environment. I was told by everybody around me that it was improper to rejoice in my talents and expeditious to work diligently on improving those things about me that others found below the norm, which I did. In school and later in work, parents, teachers, and managers put great effort into pointing out my defects and urging me to correct them. I learned that I should not fly.

At the same time, with fewer words but an intensity that pierced me to my very heart, these same people— parents, teachers, and managers—indicated their love, respect, and even awe for the hawk that lived in the center of my being. And finally, in these, my later years, the hawk has begun to win out. I have felt the lesions coming free. I have felt the wings poised to fly. I have felt my eyes clear and even blaze with the certitude of a ferocious soul. Perhaps soon I might deserve the name Hawk. But it is not yet mine. And if someday I do deserve the name, I will not take it. For I am proud of who I was and who I am. I am proud of the scars, of surviving the wounds. And I deeply love those who gave them to me. They did it because they thought it needed doing. They thought it needed doing because it had been done to them. And they gave me more. Those who inflicted the pain gave me the strength and determination to grow through it.

So my name is Crippled Hawk. What's your name?

From time to time I have told people my spiritual name and the reasons for my choosing it, then asked them to think awhile, perhaps a day, and then tell me their spiritual name. In this manner I have met Laughing Girl, Medicine Boy, Quiet Lady by the Water, Lightly Running, and Dancing Woman. These were all people I had partially known for years under their given names but came to know much more closely this way. So after you have thought about your spiritual name, try asking others theirs, one by one or in a group. You may be given a new insight into the person who has been sitting in the next office all these years.

PITY

———— ⤜✕⤛ ————

I SAW HER BACK-UP LIGHTS JUST AS I SWUNG INTO THE parking-ramp stall. After entering the ramp, I had followed her car, a safe and polite distance behind, up three levels. As she disappeared around one corner to the left, I had thought it strange that she had ignored the vast opening to the right, but since I was nearly late for my appointment, I just thanked the stars for the gift of this parking place, cut my wheels toward it, and while catching a glimpse of back-up lights from the corner of my eye, slid into the parking spot. I looked in the rearview mirror to see her car, now five feet from mine, neatly prevented from backing in by my selection of the very place she had hoped to have.

"Maybe if I ignore this, she will just go away," I thought as I busied myself collecting briefcase, pipe, keys, and topcoat. I stepped out of the truck. She had not gone away. She was standing next to her car, fury evident in every line of her body.

"I just want you to know that that is the most despicable thing I have seen someone do in a long time." With that, she got behind her wheel and drove up the ramp, searching for another parking spot.

"Great start to the day, Cowan," I thought. "Wonder what she would have said if she knew you wrote a book entitled *Small Decencies*."

There is a story told of the desert fathers, a group of fourth-century hermits living in proximate caves. A younger hermit approached one of the ancient ones with the question "If I were to seek one feeling in my relation-ships with other human beings, what should that feeling be?"

The answer was: "Pity."

I have told that story to quite a few people, and none of them like it. Some just shake their heads in disgust and turn away. Some say something like, "I would prefer that the word be *compassion*." Or "I don't find pity a very helpful emotion. No point in sitting around being sad. Why not do something?" And then they turn away. People don't want to discuss this much, which for me has become a sign that I am on to something.

I hate being pitied. I have experienced deep rage when one person reported to me that another referred to me as "pitiable" twenty years ago. "Who does he think he is, pitying me? I am no more pitiable than he is, or the next guy. I am the same as everyone else."

Which is quite right. I am the same as everyone else. I am pitiable. *Pity* is a more flagrant word than *empathy*, *sympathy*, or *compassion*. I reserve these latter words for heroes struggling with the major travails of life: cancer, poverty, blindness. *Pity* is the proper word for myself and others struggling with things that do not matter as if they matter, puffed up with the importance of our own felt needs and wounded to the heart, not with the swords of disaster but with the pins of inconvenience.

I have come to appreciate the emotion of pity. It gives me a more favorable and useful emotional choice.

He sweeps into the room in his seven-hundred-dollar suit, crisply laundered shirt, and perfectly matched tie, ruining with his enthusiastic greeting five ongoing con-versations. He demands the seat of prominence and begins the meeting with a stupid, slightly sexist com-ment, glowing in the dutiful laughter it provokes. Shall I feel anger at his stupidity, or pity for whatever it is that drives this man to attempt to place himself above others?

His fat belly twitches in the swivel chair as he explains that he cannot do what needs to be done because too many people will disapprove of his actions. Should I rage that that much gut should be gutless, or should I feel sorrow that years of corporate life have enfeebled what once may have been a proud spirit?

She cuts her Honda in front of me at the freeway exit in a last-ditch attempt to recover from passing ten cars waiting patiently in line. Shall I ride the Trooper up on her bumper and give her a little scare, or shall I meditate on the tension driving her as she juggles children and a demanding job, and give her a wave and a smile as we work our way into downtown Minneapolis?

I was settling into Mary's office along with my partner Lynn, the internal consultant. Mary was the computer guru, responsible for analyzing some data for us. Lynn began by starting to say that we needed the report by—I noticed Mary tensing, cleared my throat, and said, "Let's put no pressure on this woman today."

Lynn is quick. It was she who had told me that Mary had had a hell of a morning, having just been criticized by her boss for the style with which she brought off her miracles. "When could we have it?" became our question, and the answer was acceptable. As I headed out the door, Mary said to me, "You are trying to get on my good side. I have no good side." That's not at all true. She had once volunteered her services to rescue me from hand-counting a questionnaire that I had poorly designed. She had had pity on me, as I now had pity on her—with quite useful outcomes.

After my appointment on the day I stole the parking space, I hurried back to the parking ramp. I had this afterimage that I needed to check out. As the woman of the back-up lights had been reaming me out, where had I been standing? I climbed the two flights from the skyway system up to my floor in the ramp. I opened the door and stared at the empty space one to the left of my old Trooper. It was still unoccupied, holding about an inch of snow, not enough to deter a Minnesota car. And there, in the middle of the empty stall, were my footprints marking the very spot where I had stood as that woman cursed me out for occupying the place she had wanted.

"Lord, have pity on her," I thought, "a woman so wrapped up in her sense of justice wronged that she couldn't even see the gift from heaven that could have been hers if she would have cooled down for a second.

"And Lord, have pity on me, a middle-aged professional who numbers among his skills the resolution of conflict yet who becomes so addled at his own stupidity that he can't see the solution when he is standing in the middle of it."

What emotion fits this scene of drama without purpose better than pity?

CHRISTMAS POWER

I WRITE THIS IN THE WEEKS PRECEDING CHRISTMAS, WHILE being flooded with the introductory chapter of the Christian myth, in which the king comes in rags, power in poverty, strength in meekness. It stands in such contrast to the American myth, in which even the most altruistic of the talented seek power over others in order to ensure that good happens and power-hungriness for its own sake is accepted as a fact of life. Indeed, many of those I know who are disgusted with the manner in which power is exercised over them seek not autonomy but a better leader to tell them what to do.

At this time of year, in this country, Christians kneel before the manger, and non-Christians are forced to allow into their consciousness the story of the Almighty becoming a helpless baby. Many might wonder what good could that possibly do; how can powerlessness change anything? Will the good overcome by simply being good? Is truth its own savior without power to rescue it?

I am puzzled about power partly because of the collision of the American and Christmas myths and partly because as every year passes, I get more and more comments about my being "laid back."

The last time somebody said that was at the end of a two-hour discussion. A prospective client commented on my being laid back, and I laughed aloud. I reassured him that I was not laughing at him; everybody says I'm laid back, so I must look that way, but my experience of our conversation was that for two hours I had been intensely

active. I had been listening, figuring out the right question to ask and asking it, figuring out the right response
and giving it, figuring out how well he understood what I
could do and what words from me would advance his
understanding, trying to look through his words and
piece together how his business worked, trying to grasp
his role and relationships in it, and finally, trying to figure out how in the long run I might be able to help his
company. I may look laid back, but it's not because I'm
not busy.

I used to be saleable as a forceful lecturer. When I was
twenty-seven, I believed myself to be a great teacher, a
clergyman propounding the truths of the universe. On
one short after-Christmas vacation I stopped by the
church in Monticello to visit the pastor and instead met
the nun who administered his religious-education program. Sister Whatever-Her-Name-Was and I discussed
education for quite a while. As was only fitting a religious
woman in the presence of an ordained male, she mostly
asked questions. The closest she came to making a statement was her expression of surprise and perhaps a little
doubt that I was succeeding as I claimed in holding the
rapt attention of teenagers for fifty minutes at a time with
my eloquence. She seemed to be hinting that I might try
a less dominating approach to education, with more ini-
tiative thrown at the student. Perhaps, she implied, they
even knew something that I did not.

None the worse for wear, I left her and hooked up with
my fellow clergyman. We had a nice chat. As I was leaving, he asked if I had met Sister Whatever-Her-Name-
Was. "Lucky to have her," he said. "Doctorate in sacred
theology from Rome, doctorate in educational psychology from Catholic University, special guest lecturer at
Notre Dame, and consultant to half the bishops in the
country. Only reason I get her to come here is that she
uses my school for research."

I drove my VW Bug one mile down the highway, pulled over to the side of the road, put her in neutral, pulled on the brake, and convulsed in laughter. "You pompous ass!" I said to myself, and then I laughed some more.

So if you think me not forceful enough, don't try to reform me; I am obdurate. I have never succeeded in overwhelming anyone with charm and rhetoric without regretting my power later, when I find out what I could have learned, and understand how far we might have gone if instead of my being dominating, we had been partners.

I think the Christmas king comes in poverty because that is the only way to get anything useful done. Power overwhelms. Certainly it succeeds in changing other people's behavior in the short run, but in the long run they go back to doing whatever they originally thought was right. The other person's heart was never touched because it was never revealed. The Christmas baby says, "I am helpless. You can tell me who you are, what you think, how you feel, and I will not force you to be different than you are. But I offer you an alternative way of life. Does it touch your heart? Would you like to embrace it?"

Corporate leaders who institute sweeping change based on their power alone will one day be unpleasantly surprised by what others could have told them. Consultants who razzle-dazzle their clients into spectacular innovations had better jump to the next client before reality catches up to them. Teachers who tell adult students the right answers in complicated matters appeal to the dependent child in all of us, the child eager for mommy's breast. Intelligent students do not make it far from the classroom before realizing that they have not received adult nourishment.

This is where I stand. In the complex world in which I work, my opinion unadulterated by the opinions of others is garbage. When I have heard from others and thought about what they have told me, I will state my opinion, even forcefully if necessary. But I seldom need force. All my clients have ears. People without ears don't hire me. They need someone more forceful to ignore.

I owe a debt of gratitude to a nun who was neither forceful nor dominating. But she left me one small seed of an idea that has wrapped its roots around my soul. It is nearly Christmas, and I hear her message again: that the proud will be scattered in the conceit of their hearts. It takes a while, but it happens. The scattering of my pride started on Christmas vacation, one mile south of Monticello, and continues to this day.

HUMPTY DUMPTY

———— ✦ ————

THERE IS A JELL-O MOLD SOMEWHERE THAT IS COUGHING out the supermodern businessperson. Have you not seen this breed, who think that they know the right answer before they have seen the problem? They have properly cultured tones, remarkable syntax, excellent grammar, and use terms such as "strategy," "qualifying the customer," "TQM," and "Learning Organization" with no respect for their meaning, since they have no idea what they mean in practice.

Perhaps this situation is due to the fact that some colleges attempt to teach business as an undergraduate program. Business should be a graduate program that cannot be entered until one can prove that one has spent ten years actually working in business, preferably with a few years on the very bottom of the ladder. What is true for the student should be doubly true for the professor. What good is a Ph.D. in this strange world unless the doctor has spent a few months in the stockroom, or at least a few years sitting behind a mere professional's desk, attempting to do some good in a resistant organization?

This is said on the basis of the well-substantiated theory that you can't have the slightest idea how any business works until you have spent time working in the factory, selling shoes, groveling on commission, or staring at a down computer and realizing that your company's nearest repair part is ten states and one day away and you better find a low-profile way to communicate that to your customer, the store manager, who thinks that when your company sent you to him, you could actually fix the thing.

These supermodern businesspeople look brittle to me, like eggs waiting to be broken or Humpty Dumpty sitting on a wall. And if no one else pushes them off, I'd like to. I want to see the mascara go splat. I want to see that muscular musclehead who is pretending to be a businessman fall on his nose. I want to see that puffy, puffing powderhead deflated. I see through the brittle shell, and the inside is nothing but yolk. We have too many of them I say. American business is doomed. Humpty Dumpty will fall from the wall. The egg is about to crack. Stand clear! These cutie pies are going to spread all over the floor, and take the rest of us with them.

I was recently invited to a conference to read some sections of *Small Decencies*, my last book. I slipped in a little early to hear the ending of the last work session and get a feel for my audience. One of the participants, a neat and certain little lady in a most proper business suit, was lecturing the others, for reasons known only to God, on Vienna sausage, the kind that comes in a can. "Who would eat that stuff?" she asked her fellow participants. "What kind of people could possibly ingest those horrible little things without throwing up?" The facilitator tried to give her a gentle warning that maybe some such lowbrows were present in this group. But she was not to be stopped. "Who would dare admit it? Which of you would dare admit that you eat Vienna sausage from a can?" Nobody admitted it.

"Humpty Dumpty is sitting on the wall," was my thought. "Someday that arrogant little airhead is going to get in a position where guts are required instead of style, and when she loses, she will be most happy to eat anything, even crow, and certainly Vienna sausage."

My turn to talk came. Early in my introduction I told her that I eat Vienna sausage all the time, straight from the can. I couldn't resist. Besides, it's true. I looked at her. She looked at me. Humpty Dumpty was wobbling, but did not fall. I resisted the vicious impulse to shove again, quite aware that if I succeeded in embarrassing her too dreadfully, I would lose my audience.

I read one of my essays, and we talked about it for a while. Then I read the essay I call "Integrity," about the impact of my family of origin on my work life, particularly at times of stress. I warned them that I usually cry when I read it, and true to form, I did. As I finished, and pulled out my handkerchief to mop up the tears, I looked to my right and there sat Ms. Humpty Dumpty, tears cutting through her makeup. "Who did it remind you of?" I asked.

"My grandmother," she said, and became my hope for the future. A woman who has the sense to cry while remembering her grandmother should be in charge of a sizable chunk of business. Her subordinates will be blessed, her superiors well served, her colleagues honored, her business a better place.

Maybe Humpty Dumpty will not break by going splat on the floor. Maybe, instead of a sterile yolk within the shell, there is new life, life simply repressed because my generation taught this generation that the appearance of the shell was more important than the growth within. Maybe Humpty Dumpty will break open from the inside as women and men who love their grandmothers enough to cry in public break through the business-major façade, extend their arms to their companies, and give us what their grandmothers gave them: affection, nurturance, practical wisdom, love, and a gentle smack square on the bottom.

Am I so wrong in thinking that that is what we need?

THE SHADOW KNOWS

———————— ✦ ————————

I FORGET EXACTLY HOW IT GOES. THIS SEPULCHRAL VOICE from a radio program of my youth would ask the question: "Who knows what evil lurks in the heart of men? Who knows?" Then there was a pause, and in an even deeper voice came the answer: "The Shadow knows!"

And there was that playful song, "Me and My Shadow." And didn't we play a game called shadow tag, in which the person who was "it" tried to step on the shadows of the kids who were "not it"? It was a fun game in the sunlight but even trickier in the evening, when various streetlights at first lengthen and then shorten shadows so the argument could be made, and often was, that my shadow was there when you started but was not when I crossed the light. The counterargument was that sure, your darker shadow was on the other side, but there was still a shadow on this side.

We used to ring doorbells and then hide in the shadows as our adult neighbors searched for their callers.

I no longer hide in shadows. I don't even see them—not even my own.

I seem to have decided not to look anymore at the dark outline produced by the light, although I look more and more at the obstacle blocking the light from the shadow. I didn't look in mirrors much when I was a child and can't recall stepping on a scale, although I must have. Mom combed my hair when it was combed. Now I check my outline in the mirror for the protrusion of tummy, my weight on the scale, my complexion and beard while leaning over the sink. I have a great fascination with who I am, that person on whom the light shines, that glorious personality groomed and ready for my small public. In my shadow, that which I am not and on which the light does not shine, I have total disinterest.

In the affairs of the body, this is all right. I miss some of the fascinations of childhood by not seeing my shadow, but I will survive this. It is in the affairs of the soul that not seeing my shadow becomes dangerous.

The soul's shadow is not there because of the play of streetlights. It is there by my choice. I get to decide which aspects of myself I will consider really me and which aspects—frequently polar opposites—I will ignore.

For instance, I am altruistic. I am skilled at seeing the big picture, relationships that others do not see. I am willing to discuss almost any controversial topic while withholding judgment. And I can't sing. Those are aspects of myself on which I let the light shine. There are polar aspects that are just as true of me and that I choose to force into my shadow. I am indeed altruistic: I do things for others at the drop of a hat. I plow snow, make phone calls, recommendations, and connections. I do *pro bono* work for the church, from exercising my profession with sick parishes to mopping the vestibule. But, and I try to conceal this from everyone including myself, I hunger for a certain level of income and even more for a certain level of fame. I give generously of my talents, but my greed for praise and acceptance lurks impatiently in the shadows under the back steps.

I do focus on the big picture. But some of my moments of intense brightness occur when I choose to immerse myself in detail. Spreadsheets turn me on. I can look at a piece of writing, mine or others', and say it's all right or even good. But a focused light pervades my being when I inspect this writing word by word and fact by fact. Is this the right word? Is this the correct fact?

Nonjudgmental John has a shadow John. Shadow John judges everyone including himself with standards that would make a saint wince. Most people think I like them. There are times my wife, my confidante, wonders if I like anyone, so quick am I to pick up on flaws.

And actually, I *can* sing. I was not good enough for the choir back in the seminary, so I have chosen, with a lot of help from my old teachers, to think of myself as someone who can't sing. Six months ago in church someone in the pew in front of me turned around after the service and said how nice it was to be in front of a person with a strong voice who could hit the notes accurately. A little later the rector asked why, when I lead the service, I refuse to sing the solos when I sound just fine singing hymns with the congregation. And then last Christmas I sang the appointed solos during the midnight service. My performance was nothing remarkable, but I hit the right notes. So who is the person who can't sing?

I say all of this without embarrassment. We are all like this. We choose what to keep in the shadow. We just choose different things. For a number of years I was dean of a human relations workshop called the Creative Risk-Taking Laboratory. I gradually took over from Dick Byrd, who had invented and run the program before turning it over to me. The lab consisted of four days of mostly unstructured time during which people identified their shadow side and then practiced bringing it to the fore. The meek and mild tried being abrasive. The competent tried being incompetent. The tough tried being tender, and the tender tried being tough.

I was perpetually astounded to discover what people had kept hidden in their shadow side, as were they themselves. The hyperrational engineer displayed a warmth that drew others, particularly others with problems, to him. The tiny Lutheran housewife took on the local abusive barflies and backed them into their own corner. The gorgeous executive woman nearly pinned a man in an impromptu wrestling match. (Dancers have powerful legs, as he found when she got him in a scissors hold.) The middle-aged male corporate manager improvised the most compelling ballet I have ever witnessed. All of them were drawing on aspects of themselves they did not know they had—the shadow side.

Well, why bother? Eventually Dick and I gave up on the Creative Risk-Taking Laboratory. It took too much time to market, and the time spent marketing added up to an unprofitable bottom line. People did not come readily, perhaps because they sensed that examining and practicing their shadow side could be a frightening experience. They were quite right. Each of us has some things tucked in there that we are not eager to see in the light of day.

On the other hand, there are some things hidden in the shadow side that will work for me. If I could ever balance evenly my open-armed acceptance of all people with the critical judgmentalness that I keep hidden, I would be hurt less often by business contacts I decide without grounds to trust wholeheartedly. If I had not dismissed my ability to sing and had put some effort into it, I could have had a lot more fun.

There are some shadows that, brought to light, will stop confusing me. I want lots from life. I try to get it by giving to others and hoping that it will occur to them to give back. Frequently it does not occur to them. For some time this made me feel righteously superior. I have begun to wake up to the notion that if I will be clear on what I want and tell people that I want it and that I want it in payment for what I am doing for them, I have a much better chance of getting it. As it is, my graspiness lies just beyond the shadow line, around the corner of the house, confusing me *and* them. They keep answering the doorbell to find no one there, and then it rings again.

There are some things that at least I can stop punishing others for. That was another thing I learned through creative risk-taking. If I really hated something in others, it usually took only a few hours for me to identify that feature buried and held down in myself. My distaste for people who spend their lives making tons of money is closely tied to my regret at not actualizing that corner of myself. I can at least not hate them, even if I myself don't plan to become a millionaire.

So I find myself, in my fifty-seventh year, circling the house of my personality with a six-cell flashlight, exploring the shadows around the bushes, in the corners, and behind the steps. There are few bogeymen hidden there, and I don't plan to invite them out to play. But they are less scary with the light on them than they are when half-hidden. And then, behind an occasional bush or halfway between the house and garage, my light picks up the hidden figure of wisdom, of energy, of life. The search is worthwhile. I wonder why I didn't begin it earlier.

SMALL BLESSINGS

Small Blessings is the title of someone else's book, so I hope she will forgive me for using it as the title of a small essay. The title came to me while having coffee down at Cuppa Joe's with Art, and only later did I remember that someone had already used it.

Art has gotten himself into a bind. He is only coming up on sixty years of age but has himself in a position where he doesn't need to earn any more money. By the time this is printed both of his sons will have their doctorates. A careful saver with modest needs, Art can live on interest and some other resources for the rest of his life. We talked not about the sources of his income but about the consequences. Like myself and many others, Art has derived his identity from what he does for a living. But now he does not need to do anything, unless he feels it is important that it be done. He has some ideas about that, and over the last few years he has taken advantage of his freedom to do some things that seem to me quite important. He has aided a Russian Jewish family in putting its feet firmly on our soil. He has done quality training in India. He gave a paper at a conference in the Balkans. Not twiddly stuff.

Yet, as he looks back, he sees the impermanence of his work. "It's like sand," he says. "You look back and it has shifted." I can argue with that, and I did. Nothing remains exactly the way we did it, but nearly always, something of what we've done remains. Now, in 1993, I am still running into generations of a quality-training course that Art and I were instrumental in starting back in 1982. I do not casually dismiss a decade of influence. On the other hand, while I can point to traces of my work in the sand, I can't point to lasting monuments.

So we went on to talk about where the fun was in all of this if not in the final edifice, the closing minute. Art has just written a small book on how to avoid getting ripped off by home-improvement contractors. Its sales move along gently. He's had fun with it. He's been interviewed by the paper, has appeared on a major local talk show, and is working on getting an appearance on "60 Minutes," although it seems unlikely. He is finding joy in the process, whatever the result.

From here our discussion meandered on to the blessings of life. I told him of the pleasure it gave me the other night as I was walking out of the Superamerica store to hear the four-cylinder engine ticking in my Trooper. Ever since it passed eighty thousand miles, that motor just sings. As we inventoried our blessings, I noticed that all of them were small. And certainly none could be cast as a final event, a major accomplishment.

Mine were the new sauna in the basement, my yoga class, Ben being on the edge of playing varsity and really banging some people last night, David being nearly as tall as I am, Edith finding delight in a small compliment, the fact that I have found the thesaurus in my spell-check—all small blessings. Which brings me to another thought. Is not the large the enemy of the small, and therefore the enemy of feeling blessed? It is the large task and goal that prevent me noticing the small blessing. I do not enjoy the charm of the receptionist because I am concerned about my meeting with the president. I do not enjoy the pleasure of composing an essay because I am concerned about whether or not the book will make me famous. I do not enjoy the camaraderie of the managers' meeting because it is important to me that they conceive the correct strategy, the one I walked in the door carrying.

And yet, when I rummage back through time to count my blessings, what do I remember? Not what we did back at Honeywell in 1970 but Mike Garvey and I sitting on a log discussing our relationship around the corner from the Hopkins plant. Not the product of the day's visit to Hale Dodds at Dataserv, but the trip out the door when Susan, that most glorious woman among receptionists, refused to return the cigars I had handed her on the way in with my promise to give them up. Dataserv has poured thousands of dollars into my coffers and provided me rewarding work, yet my primary memory is of this lioness resisting my wheedlings with a definite no. When I choose to rejoice in my first book, I rejoice not at its final production date but in the moment I was surprised over lunch by a phone call from Amacom's buying editor, and standing there on chipped linoleum, I fed the baby with one hand, held the phone with the other, and invented the outline for the book on the spot.

Last summer, I took the run up to Duluth to be supply clergy at the tiny parish of St. Edward's. I came up the day before so I could spend the night with the senior warden's family and sleep in the guest room overlooking Lake Superior. I hear all about their struggles to make it, to be able to afford a half-time priest, to stop being their own janitors.

On Sunday I told the congregation this: "Ten years from now you will have two hundred and fifty families instead of seventy-five. You will have a full-time janitor, a part-time person in charge of Christian education, and the youth group. The leaks will have been plugged in the roof. A twenty-five-voice choir will have replaced the eight people singing here today. You will have here a fitting edifice, a monument to your skill, zeal, and industry. And you will be telling one another of the good old days, these very days you are living in now, when you knew one another, worked with one another, and loved one another. Every leak will be remembered as poetry. The tiny Sunday school will be remembered as a gem. The new choir will never replace the charm of the old. You will count the events of these days as blessing after small blessing. I know this, because that is what they are doing down the hill at St. Paul's, the big parish, the magnificent church, the church you have all avoided because you prefer to be here."

Which is probably why Art is losing interest in the success of his book. And I no longer care if my leadership course receives rave reviews. The blessings are in the process, not at the finish line. They are always small, which means they are to be treasured.

THE DEMONS WITHIN

———————— ✄ ————————

I WAS A HIGH SCHOOL SENIOR AT THE TIME, STANDING AT the edge of the dirt football field. That day I was not there to play. I was just killing time, smoking a cigarette, sometimes watching the intramural touch football game, sometimes chatting with a couple of other seniors, and sometimes daydreaming. A football rolled by. I looked toward the game to see if this was a live ball, shortly to be pursued by sweaty bodies. It was not, but was simply an overthrown pass. The players were returning to their huddles, leaving the referee looking expectantly in our direction, hoping for a bystander to collect the ball and throw it back.

It was about ten feet from me, and I moved toward it immediately, not running, but moving as quickly as I could while protecting the tops of my dress shoes from the playground dirt. A freshman raced alongside me, heading for the same ball. With the edge of my foot I gently tapped his passing right heel, driving his right leg behind his left, dumping his freshly showered and cleanly clothed body into the dust. His eager speed was such that he actually skidded on his side for a distance before stopping. I took a few more steps, collected the ball, and floated it downfield to the waiting referee.

Nobody saw what happened. I doubt that the freshman knew for sure that he had not run afoul of his own adolescent clumsiness. He glared at me briefly. But he was a freshman and I a senior, so he did nothing and said nothing. He headed back to the building. I suppose he needed another shower and another set of clothes.

I don't recall his name. I don't recall any further contact with him during the next years. I don't even know if I could have picked him out of the freshman crowd the next day. I would like to know his name. He was the victim of one of the meanest acts that I have ever committed in my life. With no excuse, I simply gave in to my demons.

What were these demons? The referee was a college sophomore. He was at the top of our little six-class hierarchy, and I wanted to please him. I wanted to show him and his college buddies a remarkable Cowan pass, a ball spiraling forty yards in grace back to his waiting arms. Perhaps I thought they might talk about me at the dinner table that night, make a respectful comment if nothing more.

The freshman was at the bottom of the hierarchy, and I thought him nothing but a nuisance, a fly to be demolished. I sometimes think God looked down on that act, recognized my demons, and decided not to grant me hierarchical power. I have had little of it, and perhaps that is just as well. I do not often want to have the feeling that I have when I remember that child's eagerness transformed into pain with a simple, gentle tap of my foot.

This love of power, along with ambivalence about those who have it over me and the willingness to abuse it, is not my only demon. I never pick up the paper without seeing myself in the headlines. "Man Shot While Arguing Over Traffic Situation." I have chased offending motorists in rage, risking death to vent my anger. The demons are there. What complicates this is that I do not want to stamp them out. That moment of sin was also one of my moments of grace.

Think how hard it is to realize in an instant that you

are being passed, decide not to exercise pure muscle, make gentle and firm contact with the outer edge of the foot precisely on the right heel, with the exact pressure to cause the unwary to trip himself. Smoothly and precisely, I had performed an athletic feat of grace, because without conflict, without concern for the future, without concern for what others might think, I had allowed the demon to act.

As I look back on my life, I see a few instances where I allowed the demon to emerge when I shouldn't have. But I see many more times when the demon could have saved me, allowed me to have some of the things other people have, if less of a reputation as a nice guy.

The Greek source for the word *demon*, is *daimon*, which simply means "divinity." It was the word they used for the inner force that drove them. It is the Latin word *daemon* that contains the connotation of evil, which partially explains why the Romans preferred the rule of law to the following of inner urges.

Demons are responsible for much of human achievement. I suspect that vaccines have been created because the researcher was driven by the demon of fame. I know that in business the field of quality improvement is being driven by the demon of marketshare. The lovely stucco on my house, a delight to eyes other than my own, is there because a salesman wanted to make a buck. Some of our greatest philanthropic ventures are tributes to the philanthropist's vanity, funded by his greed.

Demons must be ridden. They are the horses that move us forward. Demons must be bridled and controlled, for the sake of others and perhaps for the sake of oneself. Is there pleasure in riding a horse that is running amok?

I am sad and ashamed about what I did on that football field years ago. It was so unnecessary. The harm to that freshman outweighed any slight gain for me. His ability to fight back couldn't match my ability to oppress. I hope I never do anything like that again.

On the other hand, I will say to my business competitors, clients, and colleagues: "Keep your eyes open. I am not, nor do I plan to be, the sweetest guy you ever met."

THEM THAR'S THE RULES

———————— ✶✕✶ ————————

"THEM THAR'S THE RULES." I CAN'T REMEMBER WHO USED to say this to me. It sounds like the sort of thing that my dad might have said when kidding around, imitating some of the North Woods characters of his youth. Or maybe the phrase came from a comic book. In any event, there are times when I've wished for someone to guide me, shouting "Them thar's the rules" every time I make a false move or look like I'm about to.

A few years ago some friends of mine asked me to join them for a job consulting to the federal government in Washington, D.C. I agreed with some reluctance. Years before, I had consulted to the government, flying into Washington every other week, for a week at a time and I didn't like it much. I never understood the rules. At least, I never understood them until I had broken them. I could have used some Washington expert walking alongside me at all times, telling me the rules, keeping me out of trouble.

It seems that learning the rules shouldn't be that hard. One might suppose that any reasonable person could easily pick up on what reasonable people before him have chosen as right and appropriate behavior. But many of the rules in organizations don't make much sense. Frequently what I would think of as the sensible thing is precisely the thing that is against the rules.

I did not follow my best judgment. I returned to Washington for the job. The weather was much better than in Minnesota. The hotel was very nice. On the surface everyone involved was most amiable, but I soon found I still didn't know the rules.

After my first day on the job I was called aside by a fed who claimed to speak for several other feds, all of whom were horrified that I had appeared to contradict the department's associate administrator for organization development. When I told him that I had not only appeared to contradict but had intended to contradict, his horror was compounded. There was a rule, not normally spoken, that people with long titles were not contradicted in public by anyone with a shorter title. And there was no shorter title than "consultant."

I could spend paragraph after paragraph citing examples of the federal government's strange rules, rules that defeat the purpose of work. During my—thankfully—short years working there, I ran into rule after barbedwire rule, usually throat first and traveling at full speed. I am angry about that. But other organizations have other rules that work nearly as effectively to quell good work.

While working for a *Fortune* 500 company, I attended a week-long conference in Philadelphia. One of my colleagues, the representative from corporate staff, offered to drive me to the airport at the close of the conference. "You have a car?" I asked. I had been with him all week. There had been no need to have a car, but he had one. Corporate staff members always rented cars, because if they didn't do it all the time, then they might be questioned when they really needed one. So it cost the corporation two hundred bucks for a car that was never used. Those were the corporate staff rules.

What is it about these rules that allows their followers to be so cocksure that the way they are doing things is the only way in which things can ever be done? Why are they so sanctimonious?

Some rules are good and intelligent, and some rules that do not make sense on the surface have an underlying reason. I once read a story about a Maryknoll missionary to South America who was irritated by the rule that before climbing on the ferry he must unload his horse, place his belongings on the ferry, and then have his horse swim behind. To him it was a damn nuisance with no evident purpose. The ferry operator couldn't explain; essentially he would just repeat, "Them thar's the rules!"

So one day the missionary ignored the rules. Halfway across the lake his horse, burdened with his gear and unaccustomed to the luxury of riding high and dry with water all around, panicked, kicked the ferry apart, and treated all the living to a long swim. Most of the cargo, including half the missionary's gear, was sacrificed to the deep.

So sometimes the rules look crazy and are not. And sometimes the rules look crazy because they are. But when someone tells me that they are doing our best in this corporation, or that this can't be done faster, or with less cost, or with better quality, I want to look at the rules very carefully before agreeing.

Take, for instance, the cost of supervision. The rule has been for some time that no one can manage more than about eight professionals or eight other managers. I belong to the Episcopal Diocese of Minnesota, in which my bishop manages two hundred eighty other managers. There are some complaints about that. People feel somewhat distant from the bishop's advice and control and support. Some suggest that the bishop should only manage about one hundred other managers. But when somebody asserts that in industry the only way to do it is one to eight, I suggest that compared to one to two hundred eighty, one to twenty might be an acceptable and very cost-saving ratio. Of course, such a ratio would imply that corporate managers have as much competence and integrity as priests. Since I am both a corporate manager and a priest, let me assure you, the two groups are equally competent, equally honest, and, for that matter, equally pious. They just grew up with a different set of rules. Suggest to the church that for every eight priests they cough up the money to support one bishop, and for every eight bishops, the money for a provincial bishop, and for every eight provincials, the money for a presiding bishop, and expect to be laughed out of the convention. Suggest to the corporation that the CEO could handle about twenty divisions reporting to him if he were to allow some local control and autonomy and . . . well, better yet, don't suggest it.

No, the rules are not *always* crazy. But frequently it is the rules, unwritten and unmonitored, that stand between the corporation and timeliness, cost-efficiency, and quality improvement. Also—and this to me is even more important—it is often the rules that stand between us and a sane working life.

FLOWER CHILD,
YOUR TIME HAS COME!

MY DAD DIED OF CANCER. HE DIDN'T MIND THAT TOO much. At least, he said he wouldn't, when he was alive. He was a bit of a stoic. What he did mind was operations, chemotherapy, and tubes—so much so that, when he lay in a coma and the doctor offered life support, I had no hesitation in saying no. Dad revived for a short time, so the doctor asked him if he wanted a breathing tube. He too said no and added that he thought all this medical struggle to preserve his life had been a bad mistake. A couple of hours later he stopped breathing. The nurses who had cared for him, and liked him for his uncomplaining attitude, embraced my mother and sisters with condolences. They avoided me. I was too much my father's son to weep over the inevitable. I don't say this in pride or shame; it's just a fact.

On one visit to the emergency room, I left my dad to the ministrations of the doctors and nurses and went to read a magazine, smoke a cigarette, and drink coffee—all the usual things one does while feeling useless. I noticed the nurse supervisor, a slightly disheveled young woman, enter the waiting room. She began to work her way from one couple to another. I watched her style; the calm with which she sat; the care with which she listened; the infrequency of her comments; the evident drop in anxiety among those with whom she spoke.

When she reached me, she talked about my father's

condition. She answered my questions, told me what the medical staff could and could not do for him. Then she said, "You don't remember me, do you?" No, I didn't. "I'm Kathy Ryan. I was a student in your class in high school."

On my way home I was nearly overcome with emotion. Not because of my father's condition, which was inevitable, but because I had begun to remember the young adults of Kathy Ryan's generation and their beauty. They brought together the stated values of our civilization and expressed them in song, poetry, and action. They were the flower-child generation, calling many of us back to forgotten ideals.

I thought of Greg, who couldn't decide if he should escape the draft and go to Canada because he loathed violence or join the Green Berets because he believed in his country. He went to Vietnam and was severely wounded. While being evacuated, he jumped off his stretcher and limped back to help some friends trapped in a crossfire. He died there.

I remembered Al, the college kid who was pushing urban renewal and who described himself as not very bright but hardworking and long on integrity. He became mayor of Minneapolis for one or two terms, despite his prediction that he wouldn't last in politics.

What wonderful people! And where are they now? I've lost track of most of them who I knew then, but I have met many others since while hustling about corporate hallways.

Once she got her degree, she cut her hair short, dressed up like a corporate clone, and got a real job. She learned MBO, work-breakdown structures, budgeting, and control. Once he got his degree, he shaved his beard, put on a three-piece suit, learned to make presentations working across the chart from left to right, to use arrows instead of circles, and to express as much as possible in numbers. Talent, skill, energy, and a willingness to look quite a bit like the preceding generation have put them in positions of influence.

What is the world like in which they find themselves?

With the same inevitability of my father's cancer, the world is in a process of economic and political rebalancing. The United States is losing its economic and geopolitical supremacy—not to Russia, a nation tied up in the underwear of central planning, but to all those little nations that are underselling us in world markets. The ones that are taking control of their own rich natural resources and circumventing our military power with guerilla and terrorist warfare. The bottom line is that there will be less for us and more for them. Neither liberal life-support systems nor conservative chemotherapy will change that. It's in the cards. We can ease the passage, but we cannot prevent it.

What will happen as the real per-capita income in the United States falls? Will the haves have more (yacht sales went up during the last recession) and the have nots have less? Or will we find ways to distribute our still-sizable resources so the comfortable have less and the poor have enough?

What will happen when our corporations lose more of their markets to overseas competition? Will our employee relations become more merciless or more compassionate? Will we in industry become oriented more to the victory of the strong, or to the good of all?

What will happen as we lose our position of power in the world? Will we try to maintain it through covert war? Will we try to regain it by creating dependency? Or will we accept the reality and live with our former subjects and dependents as equals?

Much depends on what has happened to the flower children. Have their values, articulated so well in the sixties, been squeezed out of them by the press of business? If so, we will kick and thrash against the inevitable in an unseemly, painful, and ineffective fashion. Do they hold the same values they held then, tempered by the flames of the pragmatic considerations and painful trade-offs they have struggled with in the last twenty to twenty-five years?

If so, we have a good chance that our political and economic downswing will be matched with a moral resurgence—not of words but of actions—based on the applied values of the flower-child generation.

My father died. That was all right, with him and with me. It was his time to die. As the good book says, there is a time to die. And as it also says there is a time to live. Flower child, your time to live has come.

SUPPORT

I SAT IN MY CAR OUTSIDE THE METROPOLITAN TRANSIT Commission's Shingle Creek garage on a November night with snow wisping across the hood of the old Trooper. I was finishing one last pipe, but that was just an excuse to avoid entering the garage sooner than I absolutely had to. The game had not been much fun for the last two weeks.

I had been working to improve the relationship between MTC's management and mechanics, with the long-run intention of helping the maintenance division function better. After extended meetings with a group of selected mechanics, the production of a report on difficulties, and subsequent discussion with mechanics at all six garages and with management, I had finally produced a questionnaire containing about thirty suggestions for improvement. All I wanted was to distribute it to the mechanics on their shifts, asking them to fill it out and return it by the next day. This turned out to be not so simple.

The day before I began my rounds, management had put in place a radical shift in work hours and increased the number of people working nights. Some of the guys were as mad as hornets. So I trudged from garage to garage, eating their fury. My questionnaire was a reminder to them that management didn't listen. This, of course, was not entirely accurate, but try telling them that.

Night shifts were particularly bad for me. I would drive across the city to the darkened perimeter of a garage, slip in a side door, and work my way through aisles of parked and silent buses. To the office of the foreman, who often didn't know I was coming, since as my report said, communication downward works poorly. To the mechanics' lunchroom, where the hostile would be herded. To explain my task, to be hollered at about what goes on around this place. Indeed, at the Nicollet garage, where I had last visited the night shift, the union steward collected about half of the questionnaires I had distributed and returned them to me on the spot, unanswered. It was great fun.

So as I sat outside Shingle Creek, tightening my intestines to endure what was to come, I thought, "I wish Doc were here."

Doc is not a doctor. I met Doc when I entered the seminary in my freshman year of high school. He was a child with a peaches-and-cream complexion, the only nonjock in the class, who unlike most who avoided the athletic field was a force in our tiny world politic. The Doc is still with me. Now somewhat tubby and grizzled, his face surrounded with bushy white hair and beard, he is still a force in my internal world.

The Doc and I once drove a truck out of the swamps of Aiken Lake, with unlikely success. I drove; Doc was just along for the ride. It was one of those situations you don't quite know how you got into and wished you hadn't. We were working at a summer camp. I was running the camp that summer, and Doc was the camp infirmarian, which is how he got his nickname. I took advantage of my position to take on jobs I liked and avoid those I didn't. Me being me, I chose some jobs others might have avoided. For instance, I chose to drive fifteen kids, their counselors, luggage, and canoes out to the campsite on Aiken Lake using our ton-and-a-half stake truck, the *Jolly Green Giant*. Doc rode along to escape the infirmary, which contained several not-too-fatally-ill children.

The tarvey was fine, of course. The gravel road was

dirty but just its usual self. The Forest Service fire trail was a little soggy. And then I was poised at the top of a hill, looking down the ruts of the track that would take me the last mile to the campsite. It was rainsoaked.

I turned the truck off, hitched myself out the door, and explained to the counselors in the back that they would have to portage in. "Aw, come on, John. We can make it. We'll unload the kids, and if you get stuck, we'll push you out." I went back into the truck, started it up, the kids piled off, and I made it the whole mile, getting pushed out at the bottom of every hill. "Thanks, John," they said as they disappeared, luggage, canoes, and all, through the bushes. It began to occur to me that I was expected to get the truck back out without their help. Only Doc was with me.

He helped me find enough solid ground on which to turn the truck around. And then we began to work our way back. The same ritual was performed, hill by hill. I would pull up to the edge of the hill and look down over the *Green Giant*'s hood. There would be the two descending slimy ruts pausing in a mess of mud I had created on the way in, then turning sharply up a hill that clearly provided poor traction, then disappearing over the top. Throw a couple of twists in the track around trees and you have a picture of our situation.

I would say, "Oh, God, Doc, I can't do this. This is impossible. We are going to need help. Lots of help. It's too much for me."

He would say, "You can do it, John. It'll be easy. Nothing to it. Put her in gear and let's roll her out."

And I would put her in gear, scream down the hill, hit the mud pit somewhat sideways, spin the steering wheel, graze a tree, tilt up the hill, double-clutch, slam her into super-low, send clods flying out behind us, and the *Giant* would fly toward the top of the hill, where I would pause and say, "Oh, God, Doc, I don't think I can do this one.

Looks worse than the last." And he would say—well, you know what he would say.

We made it. Back on the Forest Service fire trail, which now looked like a superhighway, I turned to Doc and said, "You know, Doc, you could never have driven this truck out of there. How come you kept saying it would be easy?"

"Hey," he said, "You're right, I could never have driven the truck out of there. I can't even run it down the highway. But you're a great truck driver. You've got the skills. I just supply the confidence."

I am still sitting outside the Shingle Creek garage, and Doc is not with me. I gather my papers and head inside, where I find the foreman at his desk. I'll be dinged! He has heard that I was coming, and the troops are gathering in the lunchroom. As we start down the concrete another door opens and here comes Mike, the garage manager. I have not seen a garage manager at any of my previous night meetings. He explains, "We had a management meeting this morning and decided that while we know you can do this without any help from us, you might appreciate a little moral support, so we will be attending the night meetings at our garages from now on."

Oh, boy! Oh, wow! He didn't do a thing. He just sat there, and I handled the crowd masterfully, buoyed by his presence and the invisible support of the rest of the management team. Jan showed up at the Heywood garage the next day to ask if I might like him to attend all the meetings there, or would I find that a garage manager was in the way? "Attend! Attend!," I told him. "By all means, attend!" The next week they all gathered around me to hear the tale of my trip, offering various bits of belated but still welcome sustenance.

It sometimes amazes me how little it takes to turn an ordinary performer into a high-powered achiever. It makes me more inclined to offer the small word of encouragement, the gesture of support. More likely it is confidence rather than skill that is the missing element.

I wish for you that as you tackle the insurmountable, you have a Doc with you. You will surmount the insurmountable. And when you see another laborer struggling with the impossible, will you tell her that she can do it? If you do, she probably can.

HOW DELICATE THE ROSE

MY GOODNESS, THEY DO COME UP TO THE DOOR IN THE most ornate outfits this Halloween. The totally complete Tin Man. An instantly recognizable Snow White. And what are those called—Ninja Turtles? The complex costume is evidence of some mother working her fingers off so her son or daughter will be able to thrill the darkened-front-door crowds on the last night of October.

In the forties things were not quite so fancy for most of us. You or a relative went down to the five-and-dime and bought a mask from a supply stacked on a counter. That was it, all that was required. There were those willing to outfit their children in splendor, but they were few, and their target was not the front door but the Resurrection School Halloween party, at which they planned to collect first prize for best costume.

Liza, my grandmother, brought me to that party when I was in third grade. There were a couple hundred kids milling around sometimes wearing their dime-store masks, and about twenty primping for the great costume contest. They were lining up to go on stage when Liza pushed me forward. "Get in the line," she said. I said some childish equivalent of "You got to be kidding." She prevailed. She was sure I could win the contest, or at least place. I got into the line.

I knew what I felt. I did not belong in this line. My mask was orange, I remember that, and simple. A mask to be content with, rather than proud of. The adults were steering elegantly costumed children onto the stage four at a time. The audience was to applaud the loudest for the best, and these five would go on to the grand finale. I was desperate to improve my condition to at least one step above laughable. I reached into my pocket, where I was carrying a rattle. I tucked the handle under the mask and allowed the ball to hang down on my chest. It was my turn to walk onstage. The adult designated to guide us asked me kindly what that was hanging from my mask. "A rattle," I told him. "Oh," he said, "interesting idea." The applause for my costume was equally polite. They were probably moved by the sight of a little boy with an orange mask and a rattle hanging from it standing between Snow White and the Tin Man.

Liza, Liza, Liza, I will love you till the day I die, but why did you send me on that stage? Going naked might have been better. Did you not realize that your stubby, stout, and sturdy little grandson had feelings? Jeez, Grandma, that was a bad day in my life.

And I am no tougher now, just better at concealing my pain and chagrin. Is anyone tougher? Is everyone? Am I the only one like this? I just don't know. I think I fool people. Are they all fooling me?

I don't show my disappointment when potential clients tell me they're going with someone else. I inquire about what led to the decision, in the interest of better framing my next proposal. I wait until Edith comes home before I bleed. I do not respond to lectures on my failings by offering a little friendly feedback on what is being said about the offerer behind his back. But I'd like to. I do not come home and hide under the covers when a team-building process is difficult, when the team ruins with obstinate behavior something that has worked ten times in a row with others and then look at me with disdain as if I am the cause of the disaster. Lord, Lord, I would like to curl up with a grandmother's quilt hiding my head.

I once prepared some materials for a large meeting

Honeywell's ADG research department was holding. The management team liked the materials, all twenty pages, except for one sentence. They wanted me to remove the sentence that said that workplace relationships were "delicate" because they impacted the "delicate" feelings of people. They laughed at that. They pointed out that they were not delicate but were real men and could take the abrasions of work life without pain, fear, or anger. Now, I am not normally stubborn about one sentence. And usually, when I am basking in the kind of approval they were pouring on me about the rest of the workbook, I am amenable to almost any suggestion. But not that one. I stuck by my sentence. My salvation came from Bill Sackett, the department director, a man capable of equal stubbornness when he was determined on a point. He was willing to rescue a similar soul from losing an unnecessary battle. He told the management team to let the sentence stand. And they did, partly because he was the boss, partly because they had not cared a lot in the first place, and partly because they liked me and my work, so why not?

And partly because they really *were* delicate.

A few months later we had a hard-nosed team-development session with the same gang. One of their number, a manager normally in control of his organization, was letting the team down. His group was screwing up. The numbers said so. Worst of all, he did not seem to realize it. He seemed fuzzy, distracted, and lost. Team member after team member zeroed in on him, attempting to pin him down, their fury growing with every evasion. I let the attack run. "What is the matter with him?" I thought, "He deserves what he is getting."

We found out what was the matter with him two days later, when he was diagnosed with an extreme case of inoperable cancer. It had been sapping his strength and his attention for some time. Every man on that team con-

fided to me his guilt at what we had done to him two
days earlier. I told them that there had been no way to
know, what they had done was the natural response,
there was no reason for guilt, the business world is a
tough place, so for Pete's sake, don't be so darn delicate.
Of course, I feel guilt about that meeting to this very day.
So I say to myself, "Toughen up. Don't be so darn delicate."

Do you suppose that is why the rose, that most delicate
of flowers, surrounds itself with thorns?

When I see tough guys or gals in the business setting,
when I see hardness and frigidity, an unwillingness to
bend and be human to one another, I wonder what has
happened in these lives that makes it necessary for them
to grow a tangle of thorns to protect the rose of their
being. Everybody had a grandma, a boss, a teacher, or a
dad who put them out there to feel the pain of life. If
grandma hadn't done it, someone else would have, or I
would have myself, for life does have its painful side, and
it must be experienced if the joy is to be felt. But I think
we have a choice in how we experience it.

We can bear our own pain. We can openly admit it to
our friends and lovers, try to diminish the likelihood of
its recurrence, and move on. Or we can grow thorns and
pass our pain on to the next person we meet.

I never told my grandmother how foolish I felt as the
result of her overly ambitious expectations. She had
bought me the mask. She never understood that it
stacked up quite unfavorably to the Tin Man's costume.
She viewed it as sheer chance that he won grand prize
and I failed the first round. Years later she still grumbled
at the decision of those judges. I never told her anything
different. What is the advantage in hurting a rose?

THE BUSINESS BUDDHIST

—————— ✦✦ ——————

I NEED TO BE CAREFUL IN DESCRIBING ANY RELIGION I haven't put a lifetime into understanding. I have learned this by my reaction to those who, after a little research, think they understand my religion. (Even Joseph Campbell, the great mythologist, annoys me when he writes about my particular mythology. I hope he is not as wrong about other mythologies as he is about Christianity.) But for some time I have been deeply interested in other approaches to understanding the mystery of life, and one that most fascinates me is Buddhism. I feel confident enough on a few of its basic tenets so that when I read a newspaper report on a Zen Buddhist monastery in our community that emphasized the lotus position, hours of silent meditation, shaved heads, and rigorous discipline, I thought of calling the head monk and suggesting to him that it was all nonsense. My intent was not to insult him but to make a friend of him. For I am certain that any adept Zen Buddhist would agree that it is all nonsense. I did not call him, fearing that most Buddhists are like most Christians in mistaking the form for the substance. I suspected that my call might not be welcomed.

Buddhism sees the world as sorrowful and anybody who is bound up in the world as a pitiable person—which at first pass makes it difficult to explain why my boat bears an image on its bowsprit of a "Laughing Buddha." If things are so bad, why is he so happy? Because things are not bad, things just *are*. It is our response to the world that makes it a sorrowful place. We could be quite content here if we could rid ourselves of just two things: desire and fear.

While that may not seem an unreasonable stance for a black-robed monk, it does seem that a businessperson would not do well to root out desire and fear. If it were not for the desire for riches and their consequences, would anybody do anything at all? If a person had no fear, could she react in time to the business dangers that sneak up on her daily?

To state the case for becoming a business Buddhist: What would it be like to have things but not be tied to them? What would it be like to see challenges as possibilities and not as dangers? What would it be like to make business moves without anxiety?

One day I was walking with a fellow consultant who has always been more successful than I have in business. We were walking in a field, alongside a brook, when he suggested that we cross to the other side. "Cross?" I questioned. There was no bridge, and the brook was about fifteen feet wide and three feet deep. It was dotted with boulders separated by mild but definite jumps. Some of the rocks looked like they might move under pressure.

"Cross!" he answered, and without waiting, he began. He moved from one boulder to the next without stopping, his course very much dictated by what happened to his weight as he stepped on each boulder. As his balance shifted, so did his direction. At one point, when he didn't make it to the top of a rock, he turned and faced me, reversing himself. At another, only rapid windmilling of his arms prevented him from splashing down. On solid rocks he would pause for a moment. On shifting rocks he would lightly touch down and on to the next one before they had a chance to trip him. And he made it across, dry as a bone.

I tried. I had to. I knew I was going to get wet. I planned my course, moved with care, and ended up knee-deep in water. I squished ashore, emptied the water from my shoes. "God, I hate getting wet!" I said.

"Why?" he asked, and then, in sympathy for me in my discomfort, he jumped into the brook and stood there wet to the knees, shrugging his shoulders and extending his hands as if to say, it's just water, that's all.

There stood a Buddhist. He wanted to cross the brook dry, but he didn't care if he didn't and wasn't afraid that he wouldn't. He had stepped aside from desire and fear. He had made it. I had been filled with fear and was desperate to stay dry. I had not made it.

I have met my friend's fellow Buddhists often in business. They don't know they're Buddhists, but they know neither desire nor fear. They fail, and rather than quiver under their failure, they shrug it off. They experience success much more often than not because their senses and their minds are not crowded with the awful consequences of what could happen if they were to make a mistake.

Most people, including myself, are not like them. Most people I meet in business want success very badly and fear not having it; therefore they seldom experience it.

LOONS

EDITH CHASES THE LOONS AT CASS LAKE. SHE HAS A VERY small sailboat, a Styrofoam board with a single sail on a mast stuck toward the front. A ten-footer that half submerges if I put my weight on it. Fortunately, Edith is lighter than I am, and for her it sails. She chases the loons gently in the soft evening breeze, and she never catches them; indeed, she would be disconcerted if she did.

The loon, for those who have never heard its raucous laughter ascending and descending from lake to lake, is a water bird, family-oriented, graceful in flight and even more so resting in the waves. They do not fly as Edith approaches but quietly slip beneath the surface, reappearing a hundred yards and a couple of minutes away, as she tacks the little boat to seek their company once again.

We hear them on most northern lakes in Minnesota, for by day they are single fliers and fishers who scatter over the reaches of their domain, and by night they are lovers and maters who call to one another from wherever they have been. Edith chases a loon as it floats on a sunset lake, sending a high-pitched two-toned wail bouncing from the hills. Why this lonely, almost despairing call? And then she realizes that it is not only an echo she hears but that somewhere out there the call has been received and is being answered with the distant cry of a loon soul that can stand solitude no longer. The sound comes closer, overhead there are beating wings, and there he is, calling, listening, circling, descending, splashing by her side.

Edith can expect silence for a bit. Perhaps they will even drift apart a little, gently trilling a sound that says, "I am still here." As the sailboat slides up to them, they dive together and emerge far apart, tittering to one another, "Now what will she do? Whom will she follow?"

Edith brings the boat ashore. I help her pull it up and remove mast and sail for the night, and we sit silently on the bench, for the sun has not yet set and the loons have not yet sung. Then it begins. First one, then the other, then both together, the wild yodeling laughter of the loons spilling from their throats, their effortless voices ringing across the lakes.

When I was a child, I thought that loons were called loons because they sounded loony. And perhaps that is so. An authentic sound in people makes us uncomfortable; we sense an addled mind in the willingness to be unprotected, naked, and true to the soul, to the moment, to reality. What else should we call a water bird willing to let the world eavesdrop as his empty heart cries out for a companion? What else should we call this remarkable talent willing to let anyone hear her pure joy at being alive on this lake?

We are smarter or more foolish than that. "This organization is a house of lies," we say, and we take that as our reason to join the game. We are afraid of what consequence this or that decision will bring, but since fear is not the emotion of a real businessperson, we cover it up, mask it with a forced smile and a bland façade. Our heart floods with compassion for the deadline-trapped colleague suffocating from management disdain, but any cry for justice is held back by lips committed to disengaged silence.

I have worked with organization after organization where individuals have told me how badly they want to talk straightforwardly to one another. They have told me how much they need to have the truth spoken for the good of their business. They have told me the healthy sums that are invested in communication strategies. They have also told me why they themselves cannot begin right now by speaking honestly to the boss, the CEO, the colleague, or the clerical. "He wouldn't understand." "It would mean my job." "Her feelings would be hurt."

I have no idea how any strategy for communication will have any success unless one decides to say what is in one's mind. We can play games forever and draw diagrams around the equator. But useful communication will not start without someone telling the truth. There is good news in this: Commitment to telling the truth will make communication possible.

Edith chases loons on Cass Lake. I chase loons in corporations—just as she does, mostly for the fun of it. My job is the creation of loony, authentic, truth-speaking corporations. My hobby is finding the loons that are already there, because I enjoy them.

And they *are* there! They're floating comfortably on stormy waves, gliding over the surface, raucously wrestling with the problems they face. The first hint that I will meet a loon is the tentativeness with which he is invited to our meeting. "A real character," the tacticians will tell me. "A bit of a loose cannon." "Hope she is not too disruptive." "You'll like him, I think," the perceptive people will say. And I do like him. Not at the start, when the loon bounces off the sides of my carefully laid plan, points with mirth to some underlying assumptions that are just dead wrong, or cackles at the next step, which is destined to mire us forever. I wince with everybody else until the moment when the suggestions flow freely not only from the loon but from everyone else, for this looniness thing is catching.

I have met loons on every level of the hierarchy. Business-wise loons migrate to the top as easily as anyone else, and not-so-business-wise loons migrate to wherever they belong, from director to mechanic, from human resources to plant maintenance. They are comfortable on any lake that might be defined as theirs. And they are comfortable in their skins, sealed within their own feathers from the disapproving rain of those who are afraid to be loons.

I suggest to those who want a more authentic workplace, one where truth and honesty prevail, the facts are available, and the feelings are on the surface, don't waste your money on grand strategies. Just talk the truth. Pour out what is in your heart and mind, and listen to and encourage the faint call of others willing to splash down beside you. It won't take long before the loons own the lake.

A QUIET ROOM

OUR UPSTAIRS IS A PERFECT SQUARE, YIELDING FIVE ROOMS, one being the bathroom. In 1978 the largest room became Edith's and mine because there were two of us, and the smallest became her room because she felt that every woman should have a room of her own. This left two rooms, one quite large and one somewhat smaller. Benjamin lay claim to the smaller, adamantly, ferociously. Since he was four and David two, he prevailed. Why he would want the smaller room still eludes me.

He had always been willful, from the times when I would try to divert him from toddling up to other peoples' front doors to play on their stoops to the times when we fought about when to leave for hockey practice to the day he walked onto a college campus and said that despite the three-hour drive he already could tell that he didn't want to go there and had no intention of wasting his time with the official tour.

He is a hermit. He took root in that room. For the last few years we would go on vacation and leave him behind. He didn't want to go. Not for him, some other place, some other schedule, other companions. We left him retiring to his room and came back to find him still circling on a short radius around it. He needed no leash. His return was guaranteed. The cave attracted him.

Now he is gone. He's just checked out for college. It's only across the river and fifteen minutes away, but he has gone to live there. When the door bangs open at three this afternoon, I no longer have to shout, "Who's that?"

It will be Dave, not Ben. Hyperresponsible Ben. I can tell when Ben was the last one in: All lights are out and even the door to the basement is locked. He has arguments with himself, while I listen on, about what is all right to do. "No, no, Ben, go ahead, do what you want."

"Well, I got a right to!"

"Sure you do, go ahead."

"Well, let me tell you why I got a right to."

"No, don't bother, go ahead."

"But. . . ."

He is going across the river because Augsburg College offers standards, structure, support, and sports. He is building a new cave on the sixth floor of one of their residence buildings, and I am sitting over here reflecting on the last eighteen years, from the time when I had to pick him up to feel that bristly red head against my cheek to now, when a one-arm squeeze from him adjusts my vertebrae.

He will play hockey over there, and I remember the first game of his high school freshman season when his speed got him on the ice in a short-handed situation. He and the senior star came down on two defensemen. Ben cut from right to left, parking the puck five feet from the goal for his partner to shoot. The star drew his stick back for a slap shot, accelerated it forward, and instead of shooting, tapped the puck across the front of the net to where Ben was now swiftly returning from left to right into the play. He buried that puck. Damn near slammed it through the back of the net. He couldn't believe it. It was his first game, first opportunity, first shot, and he scored.

"Hey there, big guy!" I would say during the high school years, and he would tell me what his plans were, what teacher was a pain, what affront he had not endured. I will always remember the big day when he told me he had decided school was no longer a matter of getting by but was now a matter of excellence.

His friends would troop by, thundering upstairs to play Nintendo in his dark cavern. Scott lived in the cavern for some time while his mom found a new home for them. Now he will join Ben at college. There is Heather, who must be the prettiest girl in the class, silent for months and then suddenly talking for an hour close to nonstop. And Joe, who has broken three of my windows and the fender of my car, announcing as they leave for bowling, "Don't worry, Mr. Cowan, I'll take care of him." Take care of 185 pounds who bench-presses more than two hundred pounds and squats more than three hundred? But I do feel better, because he will take care of him. And they go out the door, the taller Joe and Ben with his athlete's pigeon-toed roll. And they go out the door, Heather futilely punching the weight lifter's muscle. And they go out the door, Ben lecturing Scott on what he should do or should have done. And I say to Edith, "That's kind of what we had in mind when we started this, isn't it?"

I start making money, and making money becomes a thing in itself. I gain the boss's respect, and that becomes important in itself. I commit to a deadline, and meeting it becomes the reason for my being. I write a couple of books and think that book writing is what makes me me. And then one day the room is empty. He will not be home. This is not home. And I remember why I have lived life as I have, and take pleasure that I have watched and helped him grow and have grown with him.

The door bangs open. "Hey, big Dave!" He swaggers into my office, the hat on backward, the muscular definition his brother envies showing through the shirt. So it goes on. This one plays a different tune than his older brother. But I am happy to hear it. Soon both rooms will be quiet. But I tell you, as those bodies hulk out the door in pursuit of the future, my skates shower stopping spray, I lift my stick into the air, turn to Edith and shout, "Hey girl, we've scored!" All the other tasks—our professions, our friends, our toys and games—are but preliminary to scoring this goal.

We have only a little time to dance, for soon the referee's whistle blows, and Edith and I skate to center ice, for it's not over, perhaps it's never over. They have not really finished. The scorekeeper racks one up on the board. The linesman digs the puck out of the back of the net, the referee waits to start the play again. But then, that is very much all right too.

ABOUT THE AUTHOR

TO UNDERSTAND JOHN COWAN, WHICH HE HIMSELF HAS been struggling to do for fifty-seven years, it is perhaps best to begin when he was in third grade, sitting in a pew at Resurrection Roman Catholic Church in Minneapolis, deciding to become a priest. He has pretty much stuck to that decision ever since, although it may have been difficult at times for anyone else to realize that. Presently he is a priest of the Episcopal Diocese of Minnesota, although the last time he served in a parish was twenty-three years ago, as a Roman Catholic priest.

In the meantime he has earned his living by working in corporations, by consulting to business and government entities, and by writing. Writing has been a great relief, since he has always felt that what priests are supposed to do is understand life at a somewhat deeper level than most people take the time to do and then communicate this understanding to others. Books make most satisfying pulpits. They pay better than parishes, they reach a broader audience, and the annoyed recipient has much more difficulty finding the preacher to give him a little feedback, which allows the preacher to assume that everybody who bought the book is pleased. He has written three books, *The Self-Reliant Manager* (Amacom, 1977), *Small Decencies* (HarperBusiness, 1992), and *The Common Table* (HarperBusiness), 1993.

In 1972 he married Edith Meissner, the only woman who did not have the good sense to leave him to his preoccupation with ideas and who to this day continually annoys him by trying to focus his attention on the details of life. This, of course, has been his salvation, but what rewards she finds in this task are beyond the ken of most people who know them, many of whom are of the opinion that John's one redeeming feature is Edith. They have two sons, Benjamin and David, who continually enter these books as heroes of no small proportion. They may not be as good as they are described, but the author is at least honest in his inaccuracy; these are the children he *thinks* he has.

Some years ago his friend Carroll Houle, a man doing something really useful with his life as a Maryknoll missionary in Africa, said that he enjoyed hearing the author tell stories in which he, Carroll, had been involved. It gave him a new perspective on what had happened. He had never thought to see things quite that way John tells them. Not that the author exaggerates, exactly, but he tends to see things with a little more drama than Carroll does. Mr. Cowan is willing to confess that his memory is a wellspring of unusual proportion but will stand by the essential veracity of every word he has put on these pages. And he will remind Father Houle that a man who thinks spending thirty years in the African bush is no big deal is not the best judge of what is dramatic and what is not. Which brings us to one last point about this author, and that is that while he may not notice dust and decay in his surroundings, he is most alert to really good stories when they happen eight and a half feet in front of his rather prominent nose. He always has been and, he hopes, always will be.

He is very willing to receive inquiries about his consulting services, workshops, and newsletter at his office address:

John Cowan
1498 Goodrich
St. Paul, MN 55105